This is your 6

Thanks for staying with us.

Published by
King Publishers

KP

2900 Redmont Park Circle
Birmingham, Alabama 35205

BILLY GENE KING

Just Get On With It . . .

Copyright 2000
Printed in the United States of America
First Edition

Cover Design *by* **Phoenix D. Collins**

Layout Design *by* **Pamela L. Blaylock**

ISBN#0-9703242-0-0

Acknowledgment

Writing this book has tested my courage, tenacity, and will. I doubt that I would have finished it without the enormous assistance of Phoenix Collins. She gave me encouragement when I drifted, and she pushed me when I had doubts.

Phoenix not only provided continuous motivation, but she also put as many hours into the development of the book as I did. She edited and typed the manuscript and offered many suggestions with respect to this book and cover design.

Kathrin was, and is, the motivational and spiritual guide that keeps my mind focused.

My special thanks go to the guys that I grew up with from the Dallas Cotton Mill Village, especially Lewis Mitchell (Woosie), Dickie Wilbourn, Donald Gentry, Leo Drake, and Floyd Hardin, who helped me remember the cotton mill experiences.

A special acknowledgment to Hack, who was violently killed as a teenager. Hack provided for much of the excitement during his short life in the mill village. Much of it is covered in this book.

Table of Content

Preface

"Far better it is to dare mighty things, to win glorious triumphs, win through checkered by failure . . . than to rank with those poor spirits who neither enjoy much nor suffer much because they live in the gray twilight that knows not victory nor defeat."

Theodore Roosevelt

Element

1

Kathrin

Kathrin was an African American bootlegger and prostitute.

I first met her when I was eight years old. My soon-to-be stepfather, Louis, took me to her place on a Saturday morning on his way to pick up a half-pint of Wildcat Whiskey. He asked her if he could leave me there for a few minutes while he had a drink with a friend. He came back about six in the evening and was so drunk he could hardly talk. She convinced him to let me stay for the night by telling him that he could pick me up the following morning. I was happy that she did, because she fascinated me.

She talked to me like no adult ever had before. We sat on her porch swing and she told me about her life when she was my age. She talked about her sister, and how they had to work in the cotton fields twelve and fourteen hours a day to make a few pennies. She told me about the creek located a couple of miles behind her house, and that she would take me swimming when I could stay longer. I had no idea at the time that I would be spending much of the next six years with her.

Kathrin's house was situated about an eighth of a mile from a county highway. The road that led to it was unpaved. The house, which was a small, unpainted, weather worn structure, had four rooms: a kitchen, a living room, and two bedrooms. It also had a front porch, a back porch, and a side porch. The back porch was screened, and was attached to the small-enclosed side porch that contained a divan and a couple of chairs. Kathrin ran her business out of her home. The side porch was sometimes used by customers when they wanted privacy, and sometimes used by Kathrin for purchased rendezvous.

The screened porch had sagging, unpainted, wooden shutters, hanging on the outside. They were closed during the winter and the old pot-bellied, coal burning stove, that sat in the center of the porch would glow a rust-colored red, making the porch look warm and cozy.

In the summer there were two big fans, one at each end of the porch. The fans were not sufficient to cool the area in the peak summer months, but they kept the air and flies moving.

The screened porch had four or five old tables surrounded by straight chairs with woven bamboo seats. In the corner was another table with a phonograph and stacks of records, most of which were by blues singers, Lead Belly and Robert Johnson. There was a small bench by the kitchen door, and that was my designated seat. I sat there when Kathrin allowed me on the back porch, but never past my bedtime, which was ten o'clock.

In his usual fashion of unreliability, Louis didn't show up the next day until three o'clock in the afternoon, so Kathrin took me to church with her on Sunday morning. I didn't have a choice. She simply said, "We are going to church," and she said it in such a way that I knew I was going.

I felt very uncomfortable when we first got there because I was the only white person. I slid down on the bench between Kathrin and her sister only to feel Kathrin's elbow pressing into my side, quietly but firmly, as she said, "Sit up boy".

After the service started, I began to enjoy my first of many Sundays in an African American church. The heat and humidity in the small building would become almost unbearable in the summer months. Even though all the windows were open, very little air circulated, and everyone present was sweating and wet. The preacher would pump, weave, and slap his hands together to make a point, while pouring sweat dripped from his nose. His message was always accompanied by the congregation's rhythmic responses, in unison.

I loved the singing in the church, because that was where the spirit soared. It felt as if the entire congregation was a single body moving and swaying in harmony and one accord with the gospel music.

A few people in the congregation had small hand-held fans that were made from cardboard with wooden handles. The fans had a picture of Jesus with his hands and arms reaching upward toward the sky, and a halo around his head. His face was the only other white face in the church. Kathrin would fan herself with a wide sweep, allowing the air to move across my face too.

It didn't matter that Kathrin might have been up on Saturday night until three or four in the morning serving bootleg moonshine to customers and playing blues on the phonograph. It didn't matter that she might have taken a customer into the side porch for a few extra dollars. When Sunday morning came, it was up early and off to church. Sometimes, on the way, I could still hear the blues echoing in my head.

When Louis finally picked me up on that first Sunday at Kathrin's place, he was still intoxicated, but luck was with me, and we made it to my grandmother's house safely. Louis was supposed to keep me that weekend before he and my mother married so we could get acquainted.

My mother and Louis married a few weeks later and took a two-week honeymoon. My sister stayed with her girlfriend, and I stayed with Kathrin. Kathrin was delighted to have me stay with her, and we began a life-long unbreakable bond. In the beginning, I stayed with Kathrin for entire summers, and then entire years, with the exception of during school time.

I learned to love the blues from listening to Kathrin's phonograph. Even though I had to go to bed at ten p.m., the little shack would be moving with rhythm until dawn, especially on weekends.

By some standards, Kathrin would have been viewed as trash, because of her livelihood, but she was the most spiritual person I've ever known, and she could be very compassionate and sensitive. She never allowed compassion and sensitivity to interfere with her business. This petite woman would stand with her hands on her hips, look directly into the eyes of a big fieldhand or highway worker, point to the screen door, and order them out, when they would get out of line. The troublemaker would then drop his head and apologize or leave.

I think they all knew that in times of trouble Kathrin had the support of the entire group that occupied the back porch, if she needed it. She never did.

I was not allowed to mingle with the patrons for long periods of time, but I was permitted to visit the tables occasionally.

Some of the regulars were fun to be with; they would tease me until I got Kathrin's head motion to move on.

With all her control and firmness, she could not always hide her feelings when we had to separate. Neither could I. When I was selected, at age sixteen, to live in France for a year as an exchange student, she struggled to control her emotions. She told me that she would miss me, but it would be good for the both of us. She also told me that it was time for us to separate, because I was too big to stay with her anymore.

Kathrin's beauty was astounding. She stood about five feet, two inches tall, and at 110 pounds, her frame was slim and her skin was light brown. Her eyes were very expressive, and held sadness in their depths, but they also showed a firm resolve. She rarely smiled. I can only remember her laughing when Toby, a regular on Kathrin's back porch, would tell her a joke, or when we had our Monday night parties with her sister.

Toby worked for a farmer in the area, and of all of Kathrin's customers, he was my favorite. He would run a tab during the week, come in Saturday night and pay his tab, then start another one. He used to tell

Kathrin that he wanted to take me fishing with him, but Kathrin knew his weakness for moonshine, so she never allowed it.

Toby was a stocky man that smiled most of the time, especially when he was drinking moonshine and listening to "low-down" blues. Sometimes I would see him take out his handkerchief and wipe a tear from his eye. His best friends were Clarence, also a tenant farmer, and Robert, whom everyone called Hobo, because he used to hop trains to Nashville and Birmingham. Hobo had a scar on the left side of his face where a train security policeman hit him with a steel railroad spike. It was a wound that had never been stitched, so the scar was almost a quarter of an inch wide. Hobo had the best tales about his close calls on freight trains, but Toby was the funniest.

Sometimes when I listened to Hobo talk about hopping trains, I wondered if he could have possibly been the black man that came to my house for food years earlier, before my father died. My sister and I were playing with a water hose in our yard in the mill village when I noticed a black male walking in the alley. Our house was only a couple of blocks from the railroad, so I assumed the man was a hobo. He motioned for me, and I went to the fence to see what he wanted. He said that he was hungry, and wanted to know if I could give him something to eat. I told him I would ask my mother. Since I was soaking wet, and my shorts were dripping water, I went to the back door and yelled to my mother that there was a "Nigra" man who wanted something to eat. In a few minutes she brought some cornbread out the back door, but he had already begun to walk away.

My father heard me use the word "Nigra" and called me to the back steps. He told me that I should never call black people "Nigra". I was a little confused, being only six years old at the time. I thought the term "Nigra" was the proper term to call black people. I had heard people in the village use the word "Nigger", but I had never heard my mother or my father use the expression, and I knew that it was derogatory. At that time, most southern whites used the term "colored", because that was the word printed on the separate water fountains and restrooms in the South. But many used the word "Nigra", and thought it was acceptable. I didn't realize that I had insulted the man, until that discussion with my father.

I saw many hobos, black and white, walking in the alley during the summer. I remember my mother feeding some of them cornbread and biscuits.

This event was significant for me in a number of ways. First, I listened to what my father was saying to me, because he was not angry, and I was sorry that I might have hurt the man's feelings. The other, and most important reason, was that my father, even though both he and I were unaware of it at the time, may have made the initial opening in my heart and mind for my future association with Kathrin. He made me sensitive to blacks without being sympathetic. Consequently, my soul was opened rather than closed. Indirectly, my father deserves much credit for an essential part of my being with, and the development of my relationship, with Kathrin. Years later when I related the story to Kathrin, she said that I was more like my father than I wanted to admit. When I added the possibility that Hobo could have been the man that I unintentionally insulted, the scenario was staggering. Hobo, upon hearing the story, jokingly said that he was the man, and that I owed him much for the damages.

I have often thought of the strange combination of events that brought Kathrin and I together. It was as though my father and stepfather each played a role in this unfolding relationship, even though they never knew each other, nor the impact their actions had on me. My father and stepfather were complete opposites, both physically and mentally. Yet, it was my father who adjusted my mind, and my stepfather who delivered me.

Toby, Clarence, and Hobo were Kathrin's security, and everyone knew it. If Kathrin started having trouble with a customer, the demeanor of the three changed immediately. The smiles and laughter were suddenly gone, and their eyes would focus on the troublemaker in unison. Most of the time the look that they gave the troublemaker was all it took to restore order. I only remember one time that trouble turned into violence. I think indirectly, I was the cause.

It was late in August, on a Sunday evening, about nine p.m., when two white men and a white woman came in for moonshine. It was not out

8

of the ordinary for whites to visit Kathrin's place, especially on Sundays. I was sitting with Hobo, Toby, and Clarence, but when the new group came in, Kathrin motioned for me to go to my bench by the kitchen door.

One of the white men was loud, obnoxious, and already intoxicated. He began to tease Kathrin. I saw him looking at me as he said something to his friends, who were sitting across the table from him. They turned to look at me, and I knew that I was the subject of their conversation. I was beginning to feel uncomfortable.

When Kathrin came back with their drinks they ordered another round, and the drunken man asked Kathrin if I was her boy. She narrowed her eyes, observing him for a long moment, and said, "Yes". The man then asked, "What's his name?" Kathrin said, "I just call him boy". While it was true that my skin was as dark as Kathrin's from playing outside all day, wearing nothing more than a pair of shorts, they knew that I wasn't her son, because I didn't have black features and my hair was straight.

The man looked at me and said "C'mere a minute, boy". Kathrin shook her head at me, which meant for me to stay. She then said to the man, "I don't allow him to go to tables." Normally the tone of her voice would have been sufficient for the man to get the message. Even with his friends telling him to leave it alone, he shamelessly propositioned Kathrin in front of everyone.

The table where Hobo and his group were sitting became quiet and serious. Kathrin was used to being propositioned, it was a part of her business, but not in the demeaning way this man did it.

Sensing trouble, she gave me the head motion to go inside, but before I could get up, Clarence had moved in behind the man and had an arm lock around his neck. Toby and Hobo were standing over their table ready to advance should there be any retaliation. The man's face was already turning a deep red, and his eyes were beginning to bulge. The other white man hurriedly said, "We're leaving, we didn't come here for no trouble", and the three of them left without any further incident.

Occasionally, during the week, one of the county's Deputy Sheriff's would drop by to visit with Kathrin. He was a large man with a round face. Most of the time he had a jaw full of chewing tobacco. He seemed to be a jolly person, and Kathrin was always friendly to him.

Years later, I realized that he dropped by to pick up his payoff for allowing her to run an illegal bootleg operation in his territory.

He seemed concerned that I was always there when he came. Kathrin told him that she was a friend of my mother, and that she kept me as a favor to her. She also said that I wasn't there at night, and then she winked at me.

Kathrin's rendezvous were as discrete as such an activity could be. She would sometimes sit down at a table with a potential customer, and negotiate in a quiet low voice. She would have no dealings with loud or crude people. She didn't have to. Most of her customers came by during the day, before the lounge opened. Logistically, she couldn't accept propositions at night while the lounge was open, unless her sister was there to serve the customers while Kathrin was otherwise engaged. She never took anyone to her bedroom; the encounter was always conducted in the side-porch room.

Her sexual clients included both black and white men. When I realized what was happening, I had considerable difficulty dealing with it. I resented it, but not for moral reasons.

Eventually, I adjusted to her rendezvous, but I still felt insecure when they happened. Even after I grew up, I resented someone else receiving her affection.

The first memorable occasion was traumatic for me. It happened when a white businessman came by on a Friday afternoon. She told me that she would be busy for about an hour, and that I should go outside and play in the yard until she came for me.

It troubled me, but I followed her instructions and went out into the yard. As I turned to look back, I caught a glimpse of them going into the side-porch room. The man was stroking her back and buttocks as they went through the door. I was hurt, and jealous, and I pouted for several days.

Kathrin allowed me to deal with it for a while before she decided to discuss it with me. She told me that these encounters were a part of her business, and that it meant nothing to her personally. She said she had no emotional attachment or desire for these men, and that our friendship wasn't compromised in the least.

As I got older, Kathrin became more possessive toward me, especially with respect to my relationship with my biological mother. When I came home from college on breaks, both of them became a little competitive about how much time I spent with one or the other.

Kathrin needn't have worried, because I never tired of spending time with her. I especially enjoyed those hot summer months, when I was a boy, at the creek with her and her sister, swimming all day, and listening to them reminisce about growing up.

I particularly liked Monday nights at Kathrin's house, because she didn't open the back porch for business, although she would sell moonshine by the bottle to drive-by customers.

Kathrin, her sister, and I usually had a party on Mondays. Her sister would stay overnight, and we played music and ate ice cream. They would have a couple of shots of moonshine, and tell me about the mischief they got into as young girls.

Kathrin never drank when the porch was open, but on Monday nights, she and her sister would get somewhat tipsey, and the stories almost became plays, with both of them acting a part. In those days, I always looked forward to Monday. Ironically, Monday is now my least favorite day of the week.

Kathrin never apologized to anyone about her livelihood. As a matter of fact, I can still hear her rationale about being what society called a prostitute. She said she was no more a prostitute than most housewives who performed their sexual obligations for financial security from their husbands. "At least I get my pay when we finish, and I don't have to put up with no bitchin man" she would say. Then softening her tone, she would add, "cept for you, and I can handle a lil' ole squirt like you".

Kathrin certainly had an unorthodox philosophy, as well as extraordinary insight. She programmed my young mind to see things in ways that I had never thought about.

I was intrigued with her views on life and death. When I asked her if she would one day die, she said she would do so only when she was ready. She said it would take place when her essence had decided that she had experienced enough, grown enough, and that she had lived a full enough life. Then it would be time for her to move into another place, and her body would begin to go. She believed that people decided for themselves when they were going to die, even though the decision was not always a conscience one.

While her beliefs may have been unusual, they reflected her wisdom and intuitiveness. I often wished I had followed the advice she gave me when I was preparing to go to France. She told me, "Don't get too close to people, and don't let them get too close to you." If I had listened, I might have avoided a lot of heartache and humiliation.

Kathrin was the person I wanted to see most when I returned from France. I was severely depressed because of a rejection by a young French girl. It was my first real love affair, and I was devastated. I wanted as much care and understanding as I could get.

Much to my surprise, and disappointment, I got nothing of the sort from Kathrin. On the contrary, she told me to get it together, and stop feeling sorry for myself. She was painfully truthful and didn't indulge me, or allow me to whine about it. She told me that I was immature to expect anything more under the circumstances, and that I was wrong to get so intimate with someone in such a short time. She reminded me that she had warned me many times not to let my emotions weaken my will.

I was very disappointed with Kathrin's response at the time, and I felt further hurt and rejected. It was that encounter that caused the longest and deepest separation between the two of us.

When I revisit that session, I realize now that she was right. Although there was a long and difficult time ahead, she had actually started the healing process in me. I also see how courageous and unselfish she was to risk breaking the bond between us by telling me the truth, so that I could eventually get my life back on track.

I witnessed many examples of Kathrin's courageous and unpredictable actions. One of these incidents was on a Saturday night in 1967, at the Birmingham Civic Auditorium.

I had just been selected one of four "Outstanding Young Men of Alabama". The winners and their sponsors were asked to go to the rear of the auditorium for pictures. I was both stunned and delighted when I walked into the holding area and saw Kathrin there. I believe she was as shocked to see me as I was to see her. She was standing with a black couple, whom I didn't recognize.

She said she was visiting friends in Birmingham, and decided to drop by the auditorium. I knew that she didn't simply drop by, but had been watching the entire program through a window on the door. I had the feeling that she paid the people who were with her to drive her there so that she could view the event without my knowledge.

I was so overjoyed when I saw her that I ran to her and hugged her. I then introduced her to the people accompanying me. I noticed that she was nervous. I told them that I used to live with her, and that she had raised me. The attention made her uncomfortable, and she said that she needed to leave. I asked her to stay for a while, because I wanted her to meet my family, something that she had refused to do for many years. I explained that we were staying at a nearby hotel. At the time, I didn't realize what a dangerous and unusual incident.was about to unfold.

One of the security guards asked if anyone was staying at the Holiday Inn. Kathrin and I immediately looked at each other with surprise. The question seemed odd, since he was standing next to us when I told her we were staying there just minutes earlier. I told him yes. He responded with a chilling expression and told us that the police were evacuating the hotel because of a bomb threat.

I rushed into the auditorium to find my wife, telling her that we needed to go. I didn't tell her about the bomb threat.

As we hurriedly left the auditorium, I looked for Kathrin, but the guard said that she had already left with the people who were accompanying her.

I was in a near panic when I pulled my car onto the hotel parking lot and saw all the people standing outside. A policeman stopped me and asked if I was a guest, when I said yes, he informed me that the building had already been evacuated. I jumped out of my car and told him that some of my family was in the room. He assured me that they were safe, and showed me where they were. An elderly couple, who had been staying in the room next to ours, had invited them to sit with them in their car until we arrived.

This was an evening that left me drained, as my emotions swung from one extreme to another, like a pendulum; euphoria, when I realized that my resume' was being read as one of the winners; elation, when I saw Kathrin was there; and terror, as I raced to the hotel.

Threats were a sign of the time. It was not uncommon in the mid-sixties for racist fanatics to make bomb threats in protest of the civil rights movement. Violence was the order of the day in Alabama.

Reflecting on that wonderful, yet terrible night, in Birmingham, I have often wondered if the revelation of my close and special relationship with Kathrin could have triggered the suspicious series of events that followed.

Kathrin was obviously traumatized by the incident. I believe it prevented her from participating, or attending any of my campaign victory celebrations years later, when I became involved in politics.

Part II

Cotton Mill Village

An entire novel could be written about the Dallas Mill Village, but for now, a little about its history.

Dallas Manufacturing Company came to Madison County, Alabama in the early 1900s, to capitalize on low wages and the high production output of the rural south. It gave the tenant farmers an opportunity to leave the farm and get regular wages, without having to work in the fields night and day.

In order to entice the tenant farmers to move into the mill villages, the mill companies had to provide living quarters. Tenant farmers were accustomed to living in houses provided by the landowners. Even though the houses were little more than shacks, they provided a roof over their heads. In an attempt to deal with the need for housing, the mills built small communities of houses, schools, grocery stores, and a YMCA near the mills. The houses were mostly duplexes with three rooms straight back. They also established boarding houses with free living quarters for the operators, provided that they would take in boarders who worked at the mill. The combination of duplexes and boarding houses solved most of the housing needs.

Early records of mill employees show that children as young as twelve and fourteen years old were working in the mills during the 1920s. In most instances, until the mills closed, both parents worked there to earn enough money to feed their families.

Cotton mill living must have been the inspiration for a song by Tennessee Ernie Ford called Sixteen Tons where the worker owed his soul to the company store. I say this because that was how most of the cotton mill workers existed.

There were three main grocery stores in the village, the Union Store, Green's Store, and Carroll's Store. Since few mill workers owned cars, the grocery stores would send a man to the mill houses to take grocery orders each morning. He would then deliver the groceries that day, and would credit their accounts. On Fridays the workers would pay their bill, if their paychecks were enough. Sometimes they could only pay a part of it.

The Dallas Mill Company charged three dollars for rental of one side of a duplex mill house. Some of the supervisors had a complete house for their family. They were usually located across the street from the school. Even in the mill villages, there were class distinctions.

None of the streets in the village were paved when I was a child. The County would send big road scrapers to the village, in the summer months, to scrape and level the streets. I liked to smell the fresh dirt, and find the new rocks turned up after the grader went through. During the winter, the mud holes in the streets were filled with ashes from the coal burning stoves in the mill houses. The stoves not only heated the houses, but cooked the family meals as well.

Most of the mill houses had iceboxes, rather than refrigerators. The iceboxes usually sat on the back porch, with a small hose that drained water from the melting ice. An ice wagon would come through the village in the hot summer months and sell chunks of ice. The iceman kept a big tarpaulin over the ice to keep it from melting. The kids loved to see the ice wagon coming, and would climb up on the back of the wagon to get small pieces of ice from the wagon bed. Sometimes they would grab an ice pick and chop off a large piece, if the driver was away from the wagon. He would get upset if he caught them, and would threaten to tell their mamas.

The ice was delicious, especially in those hot, humid, July and August months. I remember rubbing it all over my head and chest, and watching the dirt streaks run down my body.

The main street was Fifth Street, and that's where all the village activity took place. Fifth Street is now named Andrew Jackson Way. The grocery stores, the poolroom, the barbershop, and the cafe, were all located on Fifth Street. The poolroom was located next to the alley between the barbershop and Carroll's Grocery Store.

King--Front row center

19

Two of those businesses, Mullins Cafe and the barbershop, are still located and operated in the area, by either relatives or former employees. Today, Mullins Drive Inn is one of the most popular cafes in Huntsville, and is still operated by relatives of the original Mullins family. Floyd Hardin, who came to the shop in the mid-1950s as a young man, operates the barbershop that is now a styling salon.

This little commercial area was two blocks from my house, so I would hang out there, mainly in the poolroom.

The poolroom was the cultural center of the Dallas Mill Village. It was owned by Trent Sharp, a balding, middle-aged man, with small beady eyes. His shoulders were slightly humped, as if he was carrying a load. A cigarette was always hanging out of the side of his mouth. He blew the ashes off of his cigarette without taking it out of his mouth. At the time, I thought he was ancient. Years of hard drinking, chain smoking, and dealing with the mill village boys, had made him mean and tough. He was unfriendly, and rarely spoke to anyone other than his only friend, Walt Wingo. To everyone else he just grunted.

Walt Wingo was one of the most interesting characters of the poolroom. He was probably in his fifties, and must have weighted about a hundred pounds. He could literally sit on a small stool, at the counter in a squat position, with both his feet and his butt on the stool. He smoked constantly and rolled his cigarettes himself. He wore one of those old style caps with a bill that snapped to the top. It looked a little like a beret with a snap bill; I think it was called a roadster cap.

Walt had smoked so many cigarettes that he could hardly talk. We liked to imitate him, especially his laugh, which sounded a little like a crackling wheeze. He had nothing else to do but sit and talk with the owner, Trent Sharp, and tell him jokes. They would sit there all day chuckling, smoking, and coughing.

Trent and Walt were always in harmony, except when Trent had too much to drink. When this would occur, arguments replaced the jokes. Trent would pull out his flat leather blackjack, that he carried in his back pocket, and slap Walt around. When Walt would get enough he would leave, only to return the next day with his head wrapped in gauze under his roadster cap, as if nothing happened. Then the jokes and chuckling would resume.

The poolroom was smoky with poor lighting. It had five pool tables, and a metal shaded light centered over the middle of each table. There was a long bench built onto the wall that ran the length of the building, which allowed people a place to sit and watch the pool games.

Each pool table had a slot at one end where a nickel could be inserted, or even better, if you had a slug the size of a nickel. The nickel would release the pool balls, and they would roll into a tray just under the coin slot. When a ball was sunk into a pocket, it was gone until you put another nickel in to play another game. If you were brave and discreet enough, you could catch the balls as they went into the pockets and play the ball again, but if Trent Sharp caught you, he would growl and grunt; "Boy, you ought not do that", or worse, kick you out for a few days. When this happened it was like being an orphan of sorts, all your friends were in the poolroom while you were out on the street excluded.

I never heard anyone refer to Trent Sharp by just his first name, it was both first and last name, Trent Sharp, as though it was a single word.

Absolutely no females ever dared to enter the poolroom. It was male only territory and the language alone could justify that.

It was the place where the boys would talk about the girls that they picked up at the Tick-Tock Skating Rink, and how they would "feel them up" or "make out" with them, but most of the latter was wishful dreaming.

The older guys always had a condom, or "rubber", as we called it. It would make an imprint in the wallet so that when the wallet was exposed, it showed that the owner was prepared. It was a symbol of experience, although the same rubber usually remained in the wallet for years until it disintegrated.

The poolroom was my favorite place to play hooky.

The mill village had back alleys that ran between the backyards of the houses. At the end of each backyard was a structure that housed the toilet and the coal house. The structure was divided in the middle to provide each three-room duplex with its own toilet and coal house. The coal house had a wooden sliding window, so that coal could be shoveled into it from a truck in the alley.

I always used the alley to go to the poolroom, rather than the sidewalks, because I didn't want to talk to the people who happened to be sitting on the front porches.. The alleys were primarily used for trash, garbage, and delivery.

Mill Company trucks picked up trash from the village in the back alleys. The mill people rarely used garbage cans, they just threw their trash into the alley, and the trucks would pick it up about once a month. The alleys were also used by wood and coal delivery trucks.

Pig farmers used the alleys to pick up people's table scraps and spoiled food. A fence post, usually the gate post, had a big nail with a bucket hanging on it. The bucket was referred to as a slop bucket. It was usually a five-gallon bucket used to discard table scraps. About once a week the slop man, as he was called, would drive his truck down the alleys and collect the table scraps, in huge fifty-gallon drums, to feed to his hogs. Flies, ants, and all sorts of flying and crawling insects invaded the space around the slop buckets in the summer.

Dallas Mill Village was much like the other textile mills and villages surrounding Huntsville. There were about five mills, with their associated villages just outside the city limits. Besides Dallas there was Merimack Mill, West Huntsville Mill, Lowe Mill, and Lincoln Mill. For some reason, there was always trouble and rivalry among the mill villages and their schools.

Dallas and Lincoln were probably the most competitive and violent, since they were located in the same part of the county, with only a railroad track to separate them. This track was the boundary and battle line between the two villages.

The railroad track between Dallas and Lincoln was a line that you didn't cross, unless you were prepared to fight. The fights were notorious. They were bloody and weapons such as sling shots, air rifles, rocks, and bottles, were used. There were some very serious injuries, as a result of the fights, and at least two people lost an eye.

Those confrontations lasted until the mills started closing in the early fifties. I never really knew why or how the fights got started, but they had been going on for years prior to the mill closings. I know this because

I remember hearing my uncles talking about being involved in them. I suspect it had something to do with guys crossing the tracks to pick up girls from the other village, a case of "the grass is always greener on the other side".

I do know that it was like sneaking behind the enemy lines, when we would venture across the tracks risking a severe beating. We referred to the Lincoln guys as dudes. Maybe it was because their village houses were made of concrete rather than wood. I never understood why they got upset when we yelled "Lincoln Dude" at them. I thought of a dude as something of a fancy person.

Pin Hook Creek had the best swimming holes in Madison County, but getting to the creek meant crossing the Lincoln Mill territory. The hot, humid, summer months found us sneaking down alleys and behind stores, heading for Pin Hook. One spot was called Blue Hole, and the other, Corn Hole. We shared the swimming holes with water moccasins, turtles, and old tires.

The Lincoln Mill Village was just to the east of a large stock barn where weekly cattle auctions were held. Getting through Lincoln Village, and into the stock barn pastures, without being challenged was a feat.

One memorable August day, when we had safely negotiated through Lincoln Village and the stock barn pastures, Hack, one of my mill village friends, and I had gotten within sight of Blue Hole. Anticipating the cool water, we began to run. Our speed and noise level accelerated as we got closer. Laughing and yelling, we dropped our shorts, and with our hands in the air, never breaking stride, and buck-naked, we jumped into the water still yelling victoriously; we were happy that we had made it through enemy lines. We hit the water with such force that we sank to the bottom. When we came to the surface, Hack had a water moccasin in his hand. It was about three feet long. He thought it was a rope lying on the creek bottom. When Hack realized it was a snake, he tossed it away and we continued to swim.

We were so absorbed in our horseplay that we failed to notice something even more frightening than the water moccasin. Three big Lincoln Dudes stood on the bank observing us. Their sly grins made me want to grab my pants and run, but they were standing on them. It must had been our lucky day, because all they did was tie our pants in a knot, weight them down with a big rock, and throw them in the deepest part of Blue Hole. After a few dives to the bottom, we recovered our pants, and began our daring return across Lincoln territory.

While sloshing our way home, we saw the same dudes on the other side of the creek that had tossed our shorts into the water. They hadn't spotted us.

Hack picked up a rock and sailed it across the creek, glazing the leg of one of them. Fortunately, the water was too deep and swift for them to cross at that point, so a rock fight ensued. We felt reasonably safe shouting and throwing at them until we neared a shallow area where they came across the creek after us.

We were some distance ahead and scared, so we knew they couldn't catch us. As we approached the railroad track, our boundary line, we became much braver. We shouted and gestured to them. They crossed the tracks and continued after us for a few blocks, but turned back as we got near the poolroom, because they knew we had reinforcements there.

We actually enjoyed the risk associated with crossing the tracks into Lincoln Mill Village. It added adventure and made it more than just a summer swim.

Hack was not born in the village, like most of us. He moved there when he was small. I never knew what happened to his mother; I assumed she was dead. She just wasn't there.

He lived with his dad and sister. His dad, a well-known character in the village, was loud and drunk much of the time. I can still visualize him staggering around the streets of the mill village in his overalls, and his hat cocked jauntily to the side of his head. He could be heard cursing half a block away. He verbally and physically abused Hack.

Hack is still the topic of conversation when mill village friends get together. He was one of the most reckless of the mill village guys. He would try almost anything to maintain his reputation. There was never a discernible motive for his actions. He rarely went to school, but when he did, you could look for mischief and disruption of school activities, probably because being in trouble was more desirable than being ignored.

My friend Hack was violently killed in an automobile accident in his late teens, but not before he had tested every aspect of living, and tried almost every wild adventure that a teenager could experience.

On one occasion, while walking back from the Tick-Tock Skating Rink, which was about ten or eleven blocks from the poolroom, Hack saw a car parked on the side of the street with the driver's window rolled down. He opened the door, put the car in neutral, and released the hand brake, giving the car a push to start it down the hill. All of this without anyone having a clue as to why he was doing it, until the car was already in motion. It rolled through two stop signs, and across a major intersection. Motorist were blasting their horns, and tires were squealing. Fortunately, the car slammed into a utility pole without causing any injuries.

Hack offered no explanation, other than that the owner of the car was an ass. I knew there had to be more to motivate his action, other than the sheer thrill that he got by the shock and surprise.

Hack quit school and went to Detroit to work when he was sixteen. He stayed there about six months, and came back to the village with enough money to buy an old car. Within a few weeks the transmission went out, and the only gear that would work was reverse. So true to his reputation of risk-taker, he stupefied the people in the village by driving backwards everywhere he went.

Dallas Village was not a favorite spot for city bus drivers, when they would have to make a stop.

Besides the poolroom, the bus stop corner was a good place to hang out, because of the waiting bench. It provided a place to sit. The problem with hanging around the bus stop was that the driver had to stop if he saw people waiting.

One day the driver stopped the bus, but no one got on. Everyone just stared at him. Obviously angered, he closed the doors and gave us an obscene gesture. On his return trip, that same day, Hack cabled the bus stop bench to the bumper of the bus while a lady was boarding. It took the bus a half of a block to finally stop, after a fast takeoff with the bench bouncing all over the pavement. Everyone scattered down the back alley and got lost.

There are many interesting stories about Hack and the police. One happened a few blocks from the poolroom one evening in the late winter. A police patrol car was cruising the village when they spotted a group of us standing on the corner. They slowed down to investigate. Satisfied that we were sufficiently intimidated, they began to pull away. Hack picked up a brick and tossed it through the rear window of the patrol car. Everyone catapulted into motion, disbanding in every direction.

The Dallas YMCA was located just a few blocks away, and fortunately for us, there was a basketball game in progress. Everyone got lost in the crowd, some in the men's restroom, others behind bushes, and the rest just mingling with the spectators. The police entered the YMCA and began asking questions. Of course, no one knew anything about the incident.

I rarely knew the real names of most of my friends in the mill village, they all had nicknames. In addition to Hack ,there was Woosie, Dickie, One Lung, Moose, Ding-Dong, Poolroom Joe, and the list went on. I don't know where the nicknames came from, except for Poolroom Joe and Ding-Dong.

Poolroom Joe, whose real name was John, practically lived in the poolroom from the time he could see over the tables until he joined the marines. Poolroom Joe was a skilled pool player, who later became a radio announcer and a local TV personality.

Ding-Dong got his name when he was sent, along with some other guys, into the attic of the school to dislodge the school bell. The bell would sometimes get hung on roof rafters, and the principal would send some male students to free it. On one particular occasion, Ding-Dong, whose real name is Billy, decided to venture down the attic to the girls restroom, and take a little peep through the air vents.

The view so excited him, in anticipation of the emanate arrival of girls at recess, that he hurried back to get his buddies, who were still working hard trying to dislodge the bell. They got back to the vent just in time to see the girls pouring into the restroom. The anxious onlookers, pushing for a position and straining for a view, caused the vent to give way. Ding-Dong, still clutching the ceiling vent, dropped to the floor of the girls restroom. Startled, the girls scattered in every direction, screaming and laughing. Ding-Dong got suspended and received his infamous nickname.

Each year, the Dallas Mill people have a reunion on the first Saturday in August. Many people that once lived there, or still live there, attend. I went back, for the first time in many years, August 1997, and it was a delightful experience that brought back many long forgotten memories.

As tough as the mill village guys liked to think of themselves, I saw some sensitivity that surprised me.

After the mill village reunion in 1998, a group of us stood in the parking lot for hours, reminiscing about life and experiences in the village. Finally, we decided to reconvene at the barbershop. Floyd the Barber was delighted, and closed the shop so that the discussions could proceed loud and without interruption. He picked up a couple of cases of beer to keep everyone in a jovial and talkative mood, and the fun continued.

After a few more hours, and numerous stories, we began to depart for another year. Instead of our usual jabbing, backslapping, and hand-shakes, this departure wasn't typical.

Two of these men had a history of toughness, and a reputation to match. In an unguarded moment, they embraced each other. Their spontaneous expression of emotion brought tears to their eyes, and compassion from the rest of us.

Poolroom and Butcher had grown up within blocks of each other in the village. They both volunteered to join the marines, because they wanted the most difficult and dangerous military experience available. Both were severely injured in combat.

Now, for a brief moment, the tough armor of the village male was dropped to display strength rarely shown: a genuine feeling of affection and respect for each other. They will probably whip my ass for writing this.

The duplex mill houses, the grocery stores, and the poolroom, were the foundation for a close interactive community, where children were born, played, worked, and died within its boundaries. These conditions created the unusual and unique character of one of its inhabitants. One of those was a well know village personality known as Wiley.

Wiley walked wherever he went, so it was a common sight to see him throughout the village. When I first saw him, he was strolling down the alley behind my house, on his way to work at a sawmill located a half of a block away. He was slightly humped over at the shoulders and back. A small man of about five feet tall, he was not considered to be very bright by the people of the village.

Wiley had a girlfriend that had abandoned him, and he was extremely depressed. He decided to end it all by hanging himself from one of the big oak trees that lined the streets of the village. He scheduled the dramatic event to be about the same time that his former girlfriend was supposed to be passing by. As Wiley climbed up the oak tree with his rope in hand, some of the villagers, becoming curious, began to congregate in small groups on their front porches and on the sidewalk, to see what Wiley was up to.

As soon as a good audience had assembled, Wiley, already having one end of the rope around his neck, tied the other end on to a strong oak limb about twenty feet above the ground. With a dramatic gesture, Wiley leapt from the tree limb to what he thought was certain death. However, the rope was about five feet too long, and Wiley hit the ground breaking both his legs. Consequently, instead of death, he got six months in bed with his legs in casts, and he was still without a girlfriend; a tragicomic scene, which would have fit into a Charlie Chaplin film.

Dallas Mill Village also had its heroes, sometimes a most uncommon person.

Dummy Clark was a fixture around Fifth Street in the village. He was a speech and hearing impaired man who was often the focus of bad jokes and ridicule by many of the village kids.

I never knew his first name; he was called Dummy by both young and old. He was an average sized man who always wore Khaki pants and shirts, and a brown hat.

It was difficult to judge his age, he looked the same from the first time I saw him, when I was five years old, until the last time I saw him, thirty years later.

Years of pranks and mockery must have made him an understanding person. He always smiled and winked good-naturedly at children, and politely tipped his hat to females.

To my knowledge, he was never trained to use sign language, but he always managed to communicate with gestures and lip reading.

He hung out in front of the poolroom, where he knew the village boys would be. He enjoyed the interaction. Some of the guys, that were looking for a cheap laugh at his expense, would stand behind him and make comments to him, thinking he didn't know what was happening. Even though he couldn't see their faces to read their lips, I had the feeling that he could sense who it was, because he would suddenly turn around, laugh, and point directly at the prankster.

While he was a very tolerant person, he had his limits. His always-pressed khaki pants was one of those limits.

One Sunday morning, the poolroom guys had noisily gathered in front of the poolroom when Dummy came strolling up and grinning like a fox. He was making his usual friendly gestures, and jokingly shoving the guys around. The guys would cover their mouths and playfully say "Kiss my ass Dummy", knowing he knew what they were saying. He would bend slightly forward and pat his lips and butt, sending a return message.

During this period, there were a few people in the village that were relocated there from other places. One of those was a male hairdresser. He had married a local female hairdresser who owned her own beauty shop. Their shop was located across the street from the poolroom. This was a time when beauty shops were only for women, so this man was "suspect" from the beginning. He made the situation worse by his arrogance. The only people he spoke to were the shop patrons.

On this Sunday morning, HongKong (not his real name) came out of his apartment, that was located directly over the beauty shop. He was obviously angry. His thick, black, bushy, hair looked untouched by a comb and matched his eyebrows, that looked to be an inch thick. He glared at us, clearly irritated by all the noise.

HongKong wrenched his car door open as though he was trying to pull it off its hinges, then slammed the door so hard that he got everyone's attention. The babble momentarily stopped.

Jerkily backing out of the alley, and swinging the car around, he aimed it at a mud hole just off the pavement, near where we were standing. Before anyone could move, he hit the hole, that was full of dirty water, and the spray went all over us as he sped away, satisfied that he had gotten his revenge.

I had never seen Dummy so enraged. His face turned crimson, and the veins in his neck protruded, as he looked at the wet muddy streaks on his pants.

Standing near a pile of trash in the alley, he picked up a piece of an old broomstick, that was about a foot long. Winding up like a professional baseball pitcher, he threw that stick toward HongKong's car, that was

almost a block away at the time. The stick looked as though it were flying end over end in slow motion. It descended in a perfect arch, and hit the center of the roof of the shinny, black Lincoln. The impact caused a dent, about three inches deep, in HongKong's car.

Sheer pandemonium broke out among the poolroom crowd. Everyone was jumping up and down, laughing, and slapping Dummy on the back. His frown became a broad smile, and he became a hero to the very same guys that had teased him through the years. The target of their jests had become the object of their affection and admiration.

Dummy's true heroics were yet to come. Many years after that incident, as President of the Huntsville Jaycees, I had the honor of presenting Dummy with the Huntsville Hero of the Year Award.

He had been walking along a city street, on his way home from the downtown business district. It was late at night and he saw smoke bellowing out of the windows of a house. He ran to the home, making loud vocal sounds, and frantically pounding on the door and wall with his hands. The family of five was awakened, and all of them were saved because of Dummy's actions.

I watched him that night during the ceremony. There he sat at the head table, in an ornate hotel ballroom, beaming at the crowd.

He ate his dinner as though it was a normal occasion. Every time I looked at him, he seemed to be watching me. He was, no doubt, reminiscing about those days around the poolroom in the mill village. I choked up slightly as I presented him with a huge plaque and check. I realized, when I looked at the plaque, that his name was Roy. That was the first time I knew his name after all those years. Since he couldn't verbally respond, he just smiled and nodded in every direction and hugged me.

I attempted to live away from the mill village, with my mother and stepfather, on two occasions. Once in Mobile for a few months, and once in Gadsden for a little longer. I couldn't stomach my stepfather at the time, and I managed to get back to Huntsville.

When I left Gadsden, I stayed in my grandmother's attic for a couple of months, rather than Kathrin's place. I took a summer job, at the Royal Crown Bottling Company, that was only about three blocks from my grandmother's house.

I worked everyday, with the exception of weekends, from seven in the morning until seven in the evening. I was paid twelve dollars a week. I was the inspector and rack person for the colas as they came off of the line. This was before aluminum cans and plastic bottles were used. All of the colas were stored in returnable glass bottles, and I was the first stop on the conveyer belt after these colas had been filled and capped.

The company was actually located in an old grocery store building. The front was all glass windows, so that people could stop on the sidewalk and watch the process. I felt a little like a performer.

The conveyer belt consisted of several chrome plates that were pulled by a metal chain underneath. The colas slid on a belt, lubricated with oil, so if a bottle got jammed, the belt would keep moving while the other bottles stood still.

The process started on one side of the building, with new or cleaned reusable bottles. As they traveled through the building, they would get an automatic squirt of syrup and then move to the next station, where they would get carbonated water. A machine would stamp the caps on the bottle with the carbonated water spewing over the sides. The belt would then transport them to a station, that turned them over a few times to mix the syrup and carbonated water, and put them back on the conveyer belt. At this point the mixture was highly explosive.

The next two stations were mine. The inspection station was actually two big flood lights, positioned to shine from the other side of the bottles, allowing me to see through and detect any foreign objects such as bugs, mice, or pieces of anything that wasn't supposed to be in them.

The colas were continually moving down the conveyer belt. I had a metal pin that I could slide across the frame, at the inspection station, to stop them as the conveyer belt continued to slide under them. Meanwhile, I ran to the next station to put them into their cases. As they came from the inspection station, they would advance to a large, round, moving table, and circle the table until I put them in cases, and stacked the cases on the side for the delivery truck to pick up.

I took the necks of the colas between my fingers, two in each hand. I would then slap them into the case. I would put the empty drink cases into a metal contraption where the drinks would accumulate. This contraption held two empty cases in a metal frame. When I filled up the top case, I could spin the full one to the bottom, and an empty one would be placed on the top again. I was the inspector, the case filler, and the stacker, all in one.

Sometimes it was impossible to keep up with the bottling machine. When this happened, the entire bottling process would come to a halt. This caused the foreman to verbally hammer me. His name was Bud, and he was almost as wide as he was tall.

During the inspection process, if I saw anything in the bottles, I would pull them off the line. Otherwise I would let enough of them flow through, to the round table, to fill about four cases. The round table was about twenty-five feet from the inspection station. When it got full, I would have to slide my metal pin through the frame to stop the colas. I would then run to the round table and case the drinks until I either cleared the table, or the line of colas held up at the inspection station was backed up to the capping mechanism. I literally sprinted from the inspection station, to the roundtable, and back again.

I was so exhausted, by the end of the day, that I could hardly walk. The process reminded me of one of the televised *I Love Lucy* shows, where Lucy and her friend, Ethyl, worked in a candy factory, boxing candy from a conveyer belt. When they got behind, they began eating the candy to keep up with the conveyer. I couldn't do that.

After about two months on this job, one of the colas exploded in my hand as I slapped it in the case. The explosion caused the broken bottle to slice an inch cut between my little finger and ring finger at the joint. The supervisor took me to the emergency room and I had a few stitches sewn between the knuckles of my right hand. The scar is still visible. That accident ended my bottling career, but provided me with enough money to buy an old car, which lead to many exciting adventures.

How liberated I became after I bought that old nineteen-forty-something Oldsmobile. I could load the car with my friends and go anywhere. We were limited only by the amount of gasoline we could buy. Many times we combined our pennies and nickels, and bought one or two gallons.

The car was a black four-door, with rust showing through the paint on the fenders and trunk. The top half of the grill was missing, which gave it character, and made it look like it was laughing.

This car was as much one of the guys as anyone else in our crowd. When everyone couldn't get inside, we would ride on the fenders and running boards.

We never bought oil for the car. We used the burnt motor oil from Gobby's Service Station. Gobby was also a product of the mill village, and he knew everyone in the area. His gas station was located on the corner, across the street from the poolroom. It was another popular place to hangout, second only to the poolroom. Occasionally, Gobby would get aggravated and make us leave, saying "Get the hell out of here, you're running off my customers!" He would always let us come back a day or so later.

Gobby was a short, heavy guy, with a good soul. He would give us the old burned motor oil that he had drained from other cars during oil changes, and it worked fine.

Not only could you hear my car coming from blocks away, you could see it, because of a trail of black smoke.

In terms of excitement, this car gave us daily adventure. The brakes were gone, and the steering wheel would come off of the post, if you pulled upward on it. Often, when the car was full, and the highway was clear, I would pull the steering wheel off the post, while the car was moving, and then toss it into the back seat for a reaction from my friends.

One Sunday, when returning from Hatfield, a public lake located about twenty-five miles from Huntsville, when there was little traffic on the rural highway, we were challenging each other by tossing the stirring wheel around. Accidentally, the steering wheel sailed out of the window and into a cornfield. The car pulled to the right without anyone directing it, and we managed to stop off the highway. It was already dark, and we couldn't find the steering wheel, so all seven of us had to sleep in the car. As soon as the sun came up, we found the steering wheel and continued on our journey home. The drive home was goofy and fun since nobody got any sleep that night.

The car was as notorious as the thrill seekers inside. When people at the Tick-Tock Skating Rink saw or heard us coming, they would gather at the windows to see the action.

The skating rink was a wooden structure that had two pot-bellied stoves that provided heat in the winter, but there was no cooling in the summer. The windows were simple wooden flaps that were propped open with a large two-by-four inch board. This allowed people to stand with their arms resting on the base of the window.

One night, as we came into the gravel parking area, at the Tick-Tock, we were going a little too fast, in spite of the fact that we started gearing the car down about a block away. Usually, the loose gravel on the parking lot was sufficient to stop the car when it had been geared down to a crawl, but not this time.

People were standing at the windows looking out over the parking area, as they usually did, in the mid-July heat. The car hit the building, just under one of the window openings.

Fortunately, the impact didn't injure anyone inside the building, but it was sufficient to bump a few onto the skating rink floor.

Hack received a bump on his forehead when he sailed over the front seat into the dash, but he was fine. He loved the extra attention he received because of it.

The bumper of the car was smashed against the front tire, and we had to pry it away in order to drive.

The owner told us that we were barred from the skating rink for a month, because of the damage we did to the wall, but only a week later, we were back, and all was forgiven.

This old car almost seemed to acquire a human character, or perhaps we attributed one to it, because where we were, so was the laughing Oldsmobile. It was put to the test many times, and so it stood to reason that when destiny would place us on the ultimate collision course with a freight train, the car would be there.

About seven of us were packed inside the car heading for an unguarded railroad crossing. We were traveling at top speed, which was about seventy miles per hour. A freight train was also speeding toward the same crossing. The train's whistle had been blowing ever since the engineer first spotted us.

Everyone in the car was shouting orders to me. Some were saying, "You better start gearing down, we ain't got no damn brakes." While others were yelling, "Go for it Snoddy, we can make it!" As we attempted to close the distance between the railroad crossing and ourselves, the shouts intensified. In all the confusion and noise, I gripped the steering wheel, gritted my teeth, and thought, what the hell. Then I floored it.

As the car and the train converged, neither could have stopped. Having passed the point of no return, we were then in the hands of destiny.

The highway was vibrating, and the car tires were rumbling as we hit the tracks. The train's headlight was glaring into the windows of the car and blinking between the window posts. The deafening scream of the train's whistle, was mesmerizing. A fraction of a second after our rear bumper crossed over the track, the train engine zipped past. When the sound finally faded, it left in its wake a deathly silence. No one spoke, moved, or took a breath for what seemed like a long time.

Suddenly there was an explosive release of breath, and someone exclaimed, "Son-of-a-bitch!" The dam of silence, once broken, turned into pandemonium and hysterical laughter.

This car assisted us in our liberation in lots of ways as we moved into our adolescent years. Not only did it enable us to travel beyond our mill village barriers, but it provided us with a means to get beyond some of our social barriers too. At least three of us lost our virginity in its back seat, on the same night with the same generous, friendly girl.

After my father died, most of my summers were spent at Kathrin's or at my grandmother's house in the mill village, where I swam much of the time in the creeks and rivers of Madison County.

I would like to hitchhike once again to the Tennessee river, which is located about twelve miles away, with my mill village friends, and swing out over the river on a rope hanging from a big oak tree. I remember taking my turn swinging over the river, and ducking red clay mud balls that were thrown by the guys on the riverbank while waiting their turn. When I managed to duck the clay balls, during the swing, the drop down into the water was exhilarating. However, I don't think that I would enjoy intercourse with a hot, wet, watermelon from the melon patch a quarter of a mile away, as I did then.

There was something about the sheer power, energy, and size of the Tennessee River that made it my favorite place to swim. It was a recreational haven, for those of us who couldn't afford the admission charge at the city swimming pool. Weekends would bring people, from all around the county, to the banks of the Tennessee River. They would gather near the huge Whitesburg Bridge at Farley, Alabama, that spanned at least a mile and a half across the river.

The crowd provided an audience for various shenanigans, including risky swimming challenges, and tests of courage. Sometimes even con artists could make out.

Speaking of con artists, I happened to be at the river with a few guys from the village, one Sunday in July, when one of them, nicknamed Butch, decided to work the crowd.

Butch was a small guy, about five feet, three inches tall, who weighed approximately one hundred twenty pounds. He liked attention, and was always performing.

He stood up, in the center of the area where people were lying on blankets and towels, and announced that he would dive off the river bridge for a ten-dollar bill. He said that he would do it at the third support structure, about fifty feet from the water.

No one offered him a ten spot, but a variety of people contributed a dollar, or fifty cents, etc. When the total reached ten dollars, he collected it and let his cousin hold the money.

A fisherman agreed to take his boat out to the support structure and bring him in after the dive.

Everything was now set for the performance.

My old car, as expected, was again a part of the action, hauling Butch to the top of the bridge. On the way up, he looked at me and said, "I ain't about to dive off that fuckin bridge." I said, "What about the money?" He said, "We'll keep it, but I'll have some fun first." I realized that Butch had not only conned the crowd, but me as well.

I pulled the car over to the side of the bridge to let him out. As he climbed over the guardrail, cars began to stop to see what was happening. Soon both lanes were jammed, and people were waiting for the show. He then began to play to the crowd. First he strolled to the edge of the support structure and waved to the waiting fishing boat. He then put his hands over his eyes, to block the sun, as he slowly scanned the crowd. He was obviously enjoying every minute.

When he was certain that he had everyone's attention, he approached the edge of the structure with slow deliberate movements. Holding his arms straight out to the side, as if he was going to execute a swan dive, he began stretching up and down, on his toes, with dramatic, exaggerated motions. After going through this maneuver a few more times, he stepped back for a deep breath, and another look at the crowd.

Glancing over at me as I stood at the guard rail, he said, "What are we gonna do now?" I shrugged my shoulders, wondering how we were going to get out of this predicament. I knew I couldn't move my car.

Realizing that he was in an awkward situation with no way out, I believe he decided to milk it for all it was worth. He moved again, to the edge of the structure, and began to stretch his body up on his toes and back again. His toes were now over the edge of the structure. The crowd was clearly anticipating the show, and they were in the vocal mode of oohing and ahhing as he strategically rocked back and forth while building suspense.

Suddenly, and unexpectedly, he lost his balance. His attempting to regain control, with his arms flailing and hands pushing against the air, was comical. His desperate effort to prevent going over the edge didn't work. Butch was headed for the river.

He looked like he was running. His legs were pumping, and his feet were pounding against nothing. Both arms were flapping, making the appearance of an ungraceful attempt to fly. What he was trying to do was bring his head down to avoid hitting the water flat. A little over halfway to the river's surface, he managed to achieve this objective just in time to turn the fall into a sloppy, ungainly dive. Both legs were bent and apart, but his hands were over his head to break the impact.

The spectators were silent, as they stood along the bridge railing and lining the riverbank, anxiously scanning the river where Butch went under. After what seemed like minutes, his face broke the surface of the water. He was spitting, coughing, and barely conscious. The fisherman pulled him into the boat, amidst everyone's relief and cheers. By the time he arrived, at the bank of the river, he had almost recovered. He was cockily strutting, staggering a little, and waving to the crowd.

He had fame, ten dollars, and a splitting headache that lasted for three days.

Of all the excitement and risk that I experienced in the village, I think living in my grandmother's attic was my biggest test. It was a creepy, unfinished place that didn't have heating or cooling. The floor creaked and popped all night, and I always felt that there was something, or some presence, sneaking around in the darkness. I would cover my head with a quilt until I fell asleep. It didn't matter if the temperature was 100 degrees, as it usually was in the summer, I still buried myself under the covers until I drifted off.

Getting into the attic required me to go to the back porch and climb a ladder. Many times I would come in at night and make enough noise so that my grandmother would know I was home. Then I would crawl out of the attic window and down the tree to meet my buddies that were waiting in the alley. We would hang out on the corner of Fifth Street until dawn. I would then climb the tree and crawl back into the window, relieved that it was beginning to get light.

Looking back over my life, I believe these were the most important years. The mill village provided me with an understanding of basic survival and the difficulties associated with being poor, and Kathrin gave me a balance of love and wisdom that I could not have experienced in any other way.

Element

2

French Connection

I never really understood the purpose of the student exchange program. It was a joint effort between the Board of Education and an international civic organization. I was interviewed by a joint education/citizen panel and selected to go to France for a year to experience European living. The program was especially designed for kids from a "low income" family. I misled the panel when I told them that I intended to go to college. I never really thought I could.

The exchange program provided for a college scholarship, if my year was evaluated and determined to be successful.

I was both anxious and scared. My social skills, if any, were limited. I didn't even know where France was located, but I knew that some of my uncles had served there in World War II.

I sensed a unique adventure and prepared my few personal belongings for the trip. I was excited about the airplane flight, but I wasn't prepared for such a long journey.

I declined the airline meals, because I didn't know that the cost was included in my fare. I didn't have any money, with the exception of five dollars; three from Kathrin and two from my mother. I was unwilling to part with any of it for a meal because I thought I would need it for other necessities. Somewhere over the Atlantic Ocean, I munched on peanut butter and jelly sandwiches that my grandmother made for me, but only after the other passengers had finished the meals served by the airline.

I first met my European family at Orly Field in Paris. They were very friendly. I liked them immediately, and even more after our two-hour drive from the airport to their home in Chateauroux. By the time we got there, I was much more comfortable.

I didn't sleep my first night and hardly any during the first week. I slowly became more adjusted, and began to get accustomed to my French family. I especially liked their youngest son, Paul, who was almost eighteen. Paul and I became fast friends. He was committed to teaching me French, and to seeing that I met the right girls. I could hardly wait. He always introduced me as his American brother.

I was unaccustomed to getting so much attention. Both the family, and everyone else, wanted to talk about my life in the United States. I was self-conscious about my background and often sought the privacy of the room that I shared with Paul by explaining that I had jet lag, or didn't feel well. Paul understood and gave me as much privacy as he could during the first few weeks.

On my third weekend, my French hosts took me to Paris to see all the traditional sights, The Eiffel Tower, the Arc of Triumph, the Notre Dame Cathedral, and more. The most impressive place to me was the

Louvre. We spent an entire day in the Louvre, and that was not nearly enough. I loved the Winged Victory of Samothrace and the Battling Warrior. I was shocked at the Centaur Assailing, a Woman whose head, arm, and a part of her leg were all missing.

The paintings were fascinating. I was particularly taken with the Empress Josephine and The Madwoman. I also liked Christ and the Adulteress. Mona Lisa was the best known, but it impressed me the least.

My first social experience with people my own age came during the fourth week, when Paul took me to a wine festival in the center of the business district in Chateauroux. The music was wonderful. The people were dancing and the atmosphere was very festive. We found a group of his friends, both male and female, and we drank wine and danced.

I was immediately attracted to an engaging female, Fransoui. She spoke some English, and I could manage a few words in French, but it didn't matter. We danced, drank wine, and communicated. After a while, we took a walk away from the festival and didn't come back for almost an hour. Paul was concerned, but I was in a state of euphoria.

On the way home, I told Paul how smitten I was with Fransoui and that I wanted to see her again. He said he would try to arrange it.

Halfway home I could not resist the call, or should I say shout, of nature any longer. After all that wine, I had to find a place to discretely urinate. A small rock fence, to my right along the walkway, appeared to be only four feet high and I reasoned that I could easily hop over and relieve myself. As I put my hand on the top and launched myself over the stone fence, Paul realized my intention and tried to stop me. Unfortunately I was already in the air. What I didn't know was that the wall had a twenty-

foot drop on the other side. When I finally hit the ground, I not only relieved by bladder, but I sprained my ankle, took a layer of skin off my chin and elbow, and bit through my bottom lip. I was barely conscious.

Paul, after running a quarter of a mile around and down the cliff, carried me on his back most of the way home.

His parents were in a state of panic. They called a local physician friend who assured them that nothing was broken, except maybe my pride. He bound up my ankle and required me to walk with crutches for about a week. Fransoui, to my delight, visited me every day.

When I look back at those intimate afternoons that I spent with Fransoui following my injury, I realize that I was getting more deeply involved each day. I began watching for her as soon as I got out of class, and I became anxious and upset if she was late. I was already in over my head.

We would sit in the courtyard of my French host's home and talk about our lives and families. She seemed especially intrigued with my mill village background, and my association with Kathrin.

I enjoyed listening to her stories about the French Riveria and her Aunt, who lived in Toulon. She talked about the fun she had in the summer on the Riveria.

I wanted to believe that the contrast between our cultures and backgrounds bonded us in an unusual way.

I was required to take basic French and European History as part of the exchange program, so my mornings were structured with classes until noon. Every afternoon, Fransoui came by after lunch. We stayed together until it was time for dinner, occasionally she would join us. We always got together afterwards until time to retire for the evening. She would help me with my French lessons after dinner.

We were practically inseparable during the week of my recuperation.

The entire love affair seemed like a fantasy, but I believed that it was real. I disregarded any doubts that I had allowed myself to get involved beyond reason.

In my limited experience with females, I had not known intimacy with a girl who excited me like Fransoui. She was a sophisticated, attractive, fifteen-year-old, with large brown eyes and dark hair.

She came from a family with financial means and social standing in Chateauroux. Her father was an influential businessman who had political associations throughout France.

Within a few weeks, I was obsessed with our relationship. She was constantly on my mind. I wanted to see her during the little time that we were not together.

We became sexually intimate during the first week of our acquaintance. I felt that I was hopelessly in love, and I knew that it was not a typical teenage affair. I was experiencing the most powerful feelings I had ever had for another person. Maybe it was because this was my first serious physical relationship.

I was so self-absorbed and withdrawn when she wasn't around that I became a poor guest for my French hosts. Paul was beginning to get concerned. He advised me to let things cool off a bit. I also sensed his family's concern over my spending little time there after my injuries had healed. I was usually meeting Fransoui every night and returning well after the family had retired for the evening. It was also adversely affecting my morning classes, because I was drowsy and introspective.

I wasn't experienced enough to realize that Fransoui was ready to cool the relationship when she told me that her father thought that she was seeing me too much and neglecting her other friends. She said she was restricted to one night a week and the weekend, but that her family went to Toulon frequently on weekends and she would have to go with them.

Seeing her became more difficult and I was frustrated because I didn't understand, that is until Paul confided in me. He said that Fransoui's father had discussed the situation with his father and that he had two concerns. One was that he didn't want Fransoui to get seriously involved until she had finished her formal education, and the other was that I was an American with limited family resources who would be gone in a few months.

The second reason was more painful. I again experienced that sinking feeling that I wasn't good enough to meet certain social standards, even in Europe.

Fransoui and I didn't see, or communicate with each other for three weeks. I lost touch with reality, and I did something very stupid. I went to her house to plead with her father and try to see her again. Her father was furious and threatened to call the police if I didn't leave. Fransoui made no attempt to contact or communicate with me after that.

A few weeks later, I learned that her family had sent her to Toulon, France to spend the balance of the summer with her aunt. I knew it was over, and that I had to leave France. I returned home, after only three months, even though my exchange status was for a year.

I had a warm and emotional farewell with my French family, especially Paul, whom I had come to rely upon during the difficult times. I would now have to go back to Alabama and try to recover.

When I left France, I was embarrassed and depressed. I felt that I had not only let my French family down, but that I had lost a potential college scholarship. I didn't know what to tell Kathrin and the rest of my family. I was again ashamed of who I was and where I had come from.

My disgust with myself made my decision easy. I joined the military and got lost for the next two years.

Element

3

Bottoming Out

A short time in the Air Force wasn't enough to get my life on track, or to rid my system of Fransoui.

I was still depressed, and had little interest in life in general. Ruby was ideal for my sagging frame of mind. Ruby, which is not her real name, was about ten years older than me. She was slim, attractive, and very friendly. We met at a party in Huntsville that I attended uninvited.

I liked her immediately. When she and her friends invited me to go along with them to another place to continue the party, I accepted the invitation. We went to Cedar Gap, an illegal club, and danced until three in the morning. Although it was dawn, I went home with Ruby, and stayed with her for the next twelve months.

I'm not sure why I was so drawn to her. Maybe it was because she was older, uninhibited, and loved sex. Whatever the reason, I thought the relationship was beneficial for both of us. She was coming out of a bad marriage, and I was trying to get over a painful rejection.

Ruby and I lived in five different places during that year, including Lake Shore Drive in Chicago. She was as restless as I was.

When I first met her, she was working for a used car dealer. She lived only about a block from the car lot, in a single room, and was always driving one of the dealer's cars.

She told me that she was taking care of her boss, and I knew what she meant. He would let her leave work in the middle of the afternoon, and would shortly thereafter drop by her room for a visit. I really didn't care, because I was still deeply affected by the loss of my French girlfriend.

I wanted only to hang out with someone. I knew that my mental stability was precarious. I wanted to keep my mind numb so that I didn't have to think or feel anything. She was the right person to help me achieve this state of mind.

In the short time that we lived together, Ruby had at least four jobs, that she got by being friendly with her male employers. After her car dealer job, she went to work as a waitress at a truck stop on a state highway a few miles from Huntsville. She would get off work at about ten at night, and I would drive to the truck stop to pick her up. I was usually tipsy when I got there.

Many times the place would be empty of customers and the manager and Ruby would be in the kitchen together. She always looked a little sheepish when they came out, and he didn't always get all of the lipstick off.

Ruby asked me, one night after such an incident, if I was mad at her. I lied and said no. It must have hurt her feelings, because she hardly spoke to me the entire night.

One night, when I went to get her, the truck stop was closed. The place was locked up and the lights were off. They had gone for the night.

I was upset and insulted. I didn't call her for a few days to show her that I was angry. She finally called me, and I was glad she did, because I was depressed and wanted to hear from her. She said she was sorry and that it would never happen again. It did.

She decided that the truck stop was getting boring, so she quit. All that week, we alternated between having sex and drinking booze everyday. We cried on each other's shoulder about our losses and pain, drowning in a well of self-pity to which we were both addicted. But our sorrows didn't keep us off the dance floors and out of the beer joints in Madison County.

Her next job was at a dry cleaners. Again, the owner liked her and wanted her to work from three in the afternoon until ten at night. This coincided with when his wife was not around.

During these reckless and wasted days with Ruby, I didn't see Kathrin or any of my family. I avoided everyone that I had known.

One night, when I went to pick her up at the dry cleaners, I met Raymond. Raymond operated all of the cleaning equipment in the back of the dry cleaners at night. He was a black guy who seemed too friendly. I didn't care for his style of jive talk. He kept pressing me to bring Ruby over to his house to meet his wife, listen to music, and have a few shots of booze. I didn't mind going for music and drinks, but I was not comfortable with the shucking and jiving style of his communication. I didn't know anyone that talked that way.

That night, when Ruby got off work, we went to Raymond's house. His wife seemed awkward and very nervous. She tried to be friendly, but she seemed anxious. They lived in a small house with three rooms that were straight back.

Raymond put some blues on the record player, cranked up the volume, and got out the liquor. The music was so loud that, in a short time, the main room was filled with people that were drawn there from blocks around. They were also into the jive talk. I was beginning to lose myself in the music and booze, so I vaguely realized that they were pouring more liquor into my drinks than anyone else's.

The main room of the house had a bed, an old couch, and a few straight back chairs.

I sat down on the side of the bed and watched the crowd of people jamming to the music. A large black woman, named Doris, was sitting beside me on the bed. She was so heavy that the bed sunk in the middle, causing me to lean against her. I tried to sit up, but her weight, and my inebriated state, made it difficult.

Two guys came over to me and told me that Raymond and Ruby were going to get some more booze. I was beginning to have fun and loose my sense of responsibility, so it was all right with me.

Raymond and Ruby had been gone a short while when Doris got up off the bed and asked me to dance with her. I tried to decline, but I sensed that this was not in my best interest. Doris was a smooth dancer for a big woman. She would hug me close, pulling my face into her huge breasts. She was about six feet tall, and her breasts were at the same height as my face. We were both wet from perspiration, and I was dizzy from all the liquor I had consumed.

I noticed, after a few hours and near saturation, that Ruby and Raymond had not yet returned. I asked one of Raymond's friends what was taking so long. He smiled at me, winked, and said "Awe come on boy, don't you know what's going on?" At that moment, I realized that what I had already suspected was happening.

Now I was concerned about the atmosphere in the main room. I saw more and more strangers, and they began to look less friendly. I realized the significance of being the only white in the midst of some unfriendly-looking black faces, so I made my way back to the bed and sat down to avoid attention.

Beginning to feel queasy, I decided to lay back on the bed. Suddenly Doris was leaning over me. She lowered her big body across mine, got my head in her hands, and stuck her tongue all the way to my throat. I felt as if I was being crushed. The guys thought it was amusing.

I finally managed to wiggle out from under Doris' massive body, explained to Doris that everyone was watching us, and this made me uncomfortable. She then volunteered to go into the middle room. I welcomed the opportunity to get out of the main room. When I sat down on the bed in the middle room, she was on top of me again. Someone started banging on the door, and I used the knocking as an excuse to go to the toilet, which was an outhouse in the backyard.

When I got out of the toilet, I cautiously walked around the outside of the house to avoid being seen. I got into my car and was so dizzy that I could hardly start the engine. Finally the car started, and I was in the process of backing out, when I realized that I was blocked in by a car behind me. I drove forward across a large ditch, where I momentarily got stuck in the mud. I kept my foot on the accelerator until the car came out of the ditch, slinging red mud everywhere.

I drove back to town and parked at the apartment house where Ruby lived, and went to sleep in the car. About four the next morning, I was awakened by Ruby. She was furious at me for leaving her.

She later admitted that she and Raymond went off and had sex.

Fall, with its downward sadness, began to mirror my uneasiness about being in Huntsville. We could no longer pay rent, so the time seemed right for another move.

Ruby said we could move out to the country with her mother and stepfather, but we would have to clean up our lifestyles. So we tried it for a couple of months. It turned out to be a strange arrangement. Her stepfather was a big unruly man, whom I sensed didn't like me. Her mother thought I was too young for Ruby, but tolerated my presence.

At night we would sit by the fire. Her stepfather chewed tobacco, and her mother dipped snuff. Both would spit into the fire, causing the logs to sizzle and smoke.

The house had an open airway through the center, separating two rooms on each side. We slept across the open airway in the front room.

I was always ready to go to bed early because Ruby and I could have sex, and also because there was no radio or television in their house, and I was bored with the surface conversation.

I often lay awake at night fantasizing about sneaking out of the house and pushing my car to the road without making any noise. I could then jump in, start the engine, and be gone before anyone realized what had happened.

Ruby's parents didn't work in a regular job. They got what they called commodities that the government gave out to families that qualified.

The commodities consisted of cheese, beans, meal, flour, etc. They also picked cotton during the growing season. Their house was rent-free because her stepfather took care of some cows for the owner.

I went on my first hunting trip with Ruby's stepfather, and it proved to be disturbing. He had some hunting dogs, and he loaned me one of his shotguns. We went into the field behind their house. I was walking along a path when the dogs stirred up a rabbit. It ran right in front of me and I shot it. I watched it thrash and tumble over in the field. When the dogs got to it, it was still alive. I was unnerved with the experience. That was my first and last hunting trip.

I couldn't handle living with Ruby's parents any longer so we moved up the road a few miles and rented one side of a duplex shack. It had no running water, and an outhouse. The place was filthy, and the rats watched us eat. We remained there for about two months.

One of my most embarrassing experiences, during this lost year, came when two mill village friends found where I was staying and stopped by one night to see me. Both of them had moved from the village, and had begun training in their new careers. When I saw them pull up at the shack, I was ashamed. I wanted to go out the back door and escape.

I was ashamed of what had happened to me, and of my living conditions. I wanted to stay hidden, and I didn't want to associate with any of my old friends.

I knew I couldn't run away, so I went with them on a long ride to Tennessee. We drank beer and laughed about the good times we had growing up in the village.

When they dropped me off, about three in the morning, one of my friends looked straight into my eyes and said, "Hell man, you're the only person I know who left the village and went downhill." His words rang in my ears for a while, but it wasn't enough to bring me to my senses.

Ruby and I drank our pain away, woke up feeling worse, and started again for relief. I was in a vicious cycle and I didn't care about coming out of it.

Ruby had a sister, whose husband had left to go to Chicago because there were so many employment opportunities there. I was sick of Alabama and everything associated with it, so we packed up, in an old car, and went to Chicago. We must have looked like the lowest form of southern trash in an old car with clothes stacked to the top. It didn't matter to either of us at the time.

I took a job at a steel mill, hauling scrap metal pieces from freight train cars to a testing lab. I got decent pay for the first time in my life. We partied every night. There were times when I thought I loved her, and I think she felt the same, although we both knew that our relationship was only temporary. I think we realized that it couldn't continue after a reckless night in Nashville that culminated in an automobile accident.

The accident injured both Ruby and her sister. They were required to stay in a Nashville Hospital for a week. As difficult as the accident was, it provided some redeeming benefits. It jolted both of us into coming to terms with our wasted and wanton lifestyle.

Shortly after Ruby's release from the hospital, I picked up my clothes, we thanked each other for the experience, and I put a lost year behind me.

I spent the next two restless months getting registered for college. I stayed with Kathrin for one of those months. I needed the time with her because she was upset that I had disappeared for a year without any communication.

I was ready to begin the transition for my next life.

Element
4

Transition

The commencement speaker at the college graduation class in 1962 was talking about assuming responsibilities along with other typical commencement rhetoric. I wondered what he really knew about assuming responsibilities. According to his introduction he had attended the best private schools, and an Ivy League college. He was Vice President of the University of Tennessee.

I was humbled that I was about to get a college degree, the first in my family. It was gratifying to have finished the requirements in less than three years. My skin was as black as my graduation gown, and my body was hard and skinny from working at my part-time job laying new sewer lines on the Tennessee Tech campus.

The monotone commencement speech caused my mind to drift. I wondered what had become of Ruby, the woman with whom I had spent a lost year of my life. I was sure she was fine, because she was a survivor.

As I looked at my classmates during the commencement speech, I felt much older. Not in years, because we were about the same age, It was our mileage difference that made them seem so young.

Most of the students, at Tennessee Tech, were not from wealthy families, but they were, for the most part, from good middle class families.

I wondered what they would think if they knew that just before I came here I was living in a shack without running water, and that my toilet was an outhouse in the backyard.

What a transition, I thought, from the mental and physical state of my life during my experiences with Ruby, to my graduation day.

I wondered what my first job would be, as I listened to our commencement speaker discuss the challenges of life that we would soon be facing. Here, at the end of my formal education, I was facing another major transition, and I was getting excited about it.

I was still a little sad that Kathrin changed her mind about attending the ceremonies. She had agreed to attend along with her sister, but she changed her mind the day before I was scheduled to pick them up. Her sister told me that she felt that they would be uncomfortable attending the event with my biological mother there.

The speaker's message was rolling around like echoes in my mind, but he got my attention when he talked about how fortunate we were to get a college degree. I mentally revisited those difficult college years. The entire episode seemed like a hazy dream in which I kept my mind busy, focused, and yet suspended.

I looked at my sore, callused hands, and thought about the sewer line crew that I had worked with all summer. I wondered if my physical labor days were behind me. I also wondered if the crew was working that hot day in June.

I began to reminisce about that long hot summer on the sewer lines, especially that Monday, a year ago, when I reported for my first day of work. The men were all standing by the pick-up truck that was used to transport the crews around campus. The crew of four men were all black, including George, the foreman. I had the feeling that they didn't think much of white student workers because no one spoke to me except George, and when he did, he didn't look at me.

We loaded up on the truck and went to the west side of the campus where an open ditch was blocked off with caution streamers to keep people out of the area.

My first day was an unforgettable one. The only person to talk to me was the foreman, and then only to tell me to get into the truck or to get a shovel and move some dirt.

We were given a thirty-minute lunch break at noon. Everyone brought sandwiches, except me. It never occurred to me that I would need a lunch, I didn't have any money, so when the crew started eating, I drifted away and sat on the front bumper of the pick-up truck until the lunch break was over.

I was determined to work as hard as they did. The first week was physically devastating. I could hardly stay awake in my classes. When I got to the dormitory in the evening, I would fall into bed exhausted.

I had been working for about two weeks before anyone, other than George, on the crew acknowledged me. On breaks or at lunch, when they knew I could hear them, they would make indirect comments about people who really didn't need to work, filling a job that someone else needed. I don't think they realized that I didn't even have money to buy something to eat, which changed when I got my first paycheck. But I still felt like an outsider. I knew that I was not welcome, so I tried to stay out of their way.

There were obvious racial tensions in the early 1960s, particularly in the south where confrontations and conflicts were common. I sensed the strain with the crew, especially with one of the guys, who was about twenty-five years old.

He continued to deliberately cut me off by stepping in front of me when I attempted to get on or off of the truck.

His name was Roy. On one occasion, when we were shoveling dirt out of the sewer ditch, I accidentally tossed some dirt on his shoe. He was standing behind me, and I wasn't aware that he was there. He yelled, "You Mothua Fuckua!" and swung his shovel, hitting me in the back. The blow was so hard that it knocked me to my knees, and I was struggling to get air into my lungs. Everyone stood there and watched me gasp for breath. Finally the foreman caught me by the arm and pulled me out of the ditch.

He sent me back to my dorm, reprimanding me for having provoked the incident. Roy was allowed to continue to work.

My back and shoulders were so sore, from the impact of the shovel, that I didn't sleep that night, but I was back at the pick-up station the next morning at seven a.m. sharp, and never mentioned the incident.

Before the week was over, Roy broke his silence and asked me about my back. We were working together at the upper end of the ditch, and none of the other members of the crew were around. He said, "You got dirt in my shoes and socks and I thought you did it on purpose, maybe you didn't". That was as close to an apology as Roy could muster.

The bruise was in the shape of his shovel, and I purposely kept my shirt off as a visible reminder to him.

My association with the crew had three phases. The first phase was cold isolation, and the shovel incident. The second phase was a cautious warming and a gradual change in attitudes. In the third phase, we became good buddies and lasting friends.

The uncertainty of the second phase kept me guessing. I was still cautious about warming up with them, because Roy had made me sufficiently aware of the subtle violence that was there. But the continuous challenges, that were there initially, seemed to disappear. Roy no longer delibertly stepped in front of me when getting on and off the truck. His physical aggressiveness cooled, and he began to make small talk when the others were not around.

He started kidding with me. First by talking about how skinny I was getting. My weight did drop to a hundred and twenty pounds because of the combination of physical activity, hot sun, and no lunch.

Floyd, one of the older guys, talked to me more often during this period than the others. George the foreman was the last to come around, but I suspected that was because he was the boss. He wasn't all that friendly to any of the others either.

I always took my lunch and set on the front bumper, or on the ground, a full truck-length away.

Floyd started a conversation with me as we were getting our lunches out of the truck. One day he asked, "Where do you live Billy?" I told him in the Quad, the men's dormitory. He asked, "What are you going to be when you get out of college?" I said, "I don't know". Roy answered, "A Sewer Engineer" and everyone laughed.

As I started toward the front of the truck, Floyd asked, "Why don't you stay in the shade?" I realized that he was inviting me to sit in the back with them. I agreed, and set down on the grass near Floyd, but still outside their circle.

I never had lunch alone again during my tenure with the sewer line crew.

The rest of the guys loosened up and in a few weeks they were teasing me about being black because I was so dark from the summer sun. They also teasingly accused me of being friends with them only because Roy had whipped me into shape. They jokingly added that I probably wouldn't even speak to them if I saw them on campus when I was going to my classes.

I knew they were joking, but it made me more sensitive to our relationship. I then made a point of dropping by the ditch on my off days to have some fun, mimicking George. I would give them orders and press them to work harder. I could even shuffle my shoulders and sound bossy like George. We all enjoyed the interaction.

The lunch sessions were the beginning of our real acquaintance. We learned about each other in more personal ways. I learned that Roy lived in a public housing project and had four kids. Floyd lived with his daughter, or vice versa, and she was single with two children. George lived in a trailer in rural Putnum County.

Floyd was curious about my childhood and asked questions. The others always listened, but didn't get into the discussions at first. He wanted to know about the cotton mill village. He told me he once loaded trucks in the cotton mill in Cookeville. I purposefully avoided talking about my life with Kathrin, because there was still considerable distance between us, and I didn't want them to think I was patronizing.

Roy gradually started conversing with me during our lunch breaks. He asked me if I had a girl. I told him I didn't because I had no time. Roy said, "Man you gotta have a woman, whether you got the time or not."

After Roy became cautiously friendly, the rest of them really loosened up, even George, who threatened to turn Roy loose on me again if I didn't get me a woman. He said, "You can't jack-off all the time with all them good-looking college girls around." Soon I became a part of the horseplay, and the object of many practical jokes. I then knew that I was being accepted as an actual member of the sewer line crew.

Kathrin came into our conversation one day when George sent Roy and me back to the pick up station to get some supplies. Roy deviated from the route to show me where he and some of the crew go to listen to blues and drink whiskey. It was an old run-down store building near the public housing project called *The Chicken Neck*. He said that they would take me with them sometime and show me how black folks live. I told him that I already knew, and that I had spent much of my early years in that environment. He glanced at me skeptically and wanted to know more. I stunned him with my knowledge of black blues singers and their music. When I had his attention, and felt that I could trust him, I gradually brought Kathrin into the discussion.

She slowly became a topic during our lunch breaks. Floyd wanted me to take him home with me because he had become infatuated with her. I told him that she wasn't interested, and that she had made it clear to me that she didn't want "no man". I also knew that both of us could be in real trouble if I took him there under those conditions.

By the time October came around, we were very good friends. They did something that touched me significantly. My birthday was coming the next week, and I had mentioned that I would be going to Kathrin's on that weekend. That Friday, when George gave out pay checks, he didn't give me mine. When I asked him about it, he said I would get it at *The Chicken Neck*.

I still had reservations about going to *The Chicken Neck*, because of the situation that I had encountered with Ruby. I went because I was curious, and I wanted to get paid. I had a great time, however, and I felt completely at home. They were genuine, like the people that I had known at Kathrin's.

It was one of my most extraordinary birthday parties.

By the end of the summer we were all good friends and I shared with them stories about Kathrin, Toby, Hobo and Clarence.

As my thoughts slowly drifted back to the ceremony, I couldn't help but think about their difficult lives, and I was glad that I shared those hot summer months with them.

I sensed that the speaker was getting ready to deliver his closing remarks, as I let my eyes wander out over the audience looking for my new wife and baby daughter. That brought my thoughts again to Kathrin. I wanted her to see my daughter. She never met either of my children, but she enjoyed pictures of them. She felt that it would be too confusing for them to understand our association. She should have given them more credit. I told them all about Kathrin, and they feel they missed a lot by not having the opportunity to know her personally. They are right.

I met my wife at a skating rink in Cookeville, after I had been in college about a year. She was, and is, a kind and caring woman. She actually lived in a small town about twenty miles from the campus. We met by accident, dated by accident, and later married in much the same way. Unfortunately, we didn't fit well, although we stayed married for over twenty years, much to her credit.

Dating her was risky while I was in college, because I had to drive about forty miles round trip and I didn't have a valid driver's license.

My driver's license was suspended for six months while I was in college. Of the times that I probably deserved to lose it, this was not one of those times. This incident occurred while I was actually doing something constructive. I had been studying with a classmate, who was from New York. I never knew why he was attending college in Tennessee.

He stopped by my room on a Saturday morning, one of the few days that I wasn't working on the sewer lines, and he wanted to study physics with me. We worked for a while in the dorm, and then decided to go out to the country to finish up and have a beer at a little tavern that had an outside sitting area. We only had a couple of beers, and actually spent the time studying. We did not realize what we were about to encounter as we started back to the campus.

My old Mercury car had so much play in the steering wheel that I had to turn it almost a complete revolution just to keep it in the center of the lane. This caused the vehicle to weave from side to side.

The Tennessee Highway Patrol, perhaps sensing an easy mark, followed us for about three miles after we had left the tavern. Finally, they pulled us over. One of the patrolmen directed me to get out of the car and walk the yellow line in the center of the highway, which I did without error.

As I started back to the car, I began to explain that we were students and had been studying. That was my first mistake, because college students were a continuous problem for state troopers. The second mistake came as my New York friend joined in to explain that we only had one beer. I then knew we were in real trouble when they heard his dialect.

They took us in, and we spent an unforgettable night in the Putnum County Jail. I was charged with driving while intoxicated, and my drivers license was suspended for six months.

The Putnum County Jail was a monumental nightmare. We were dressed only in shorts, tee shirts, and flip-flops, which made us automatically the center of attention in the jail. The regulars in the jail knew that they were going to have fun at our expense.

I didn't have a bed, just a rolled up, dirty mattress, without sheets or a pillow. I asked my friend to refrain from speaking to anyone except me, because I was afraid of what they might do if they heard that New York dialect.

I had read, or saw in a movie, that the jailer had to allow an inmate to make one phone call. So I asked the jailer to allow me to make my call. I didn't know who I would have called if he had allowed me to do so. After he ignored me a few times, I became indignant, and demanded my rights. The drunks in the cell were encouraging me, knowing that something was going to happen if I continued. I became more confident and outraged, and started shaking the jail door as hard as I could.

I caught the jailer's shadow out of the corner of my eye. He was creeping up the walkway with his club drawn back. I jerked my hand away a fraction of a second before his club hit the bars. It smashed against the bars with such force, that it would have broken every finger on my hand. That incident was sufficient to keep me away from the jail door.

The jailer had decided that I was a troublemaker and wanted to make an example of me. He separated me from the other prisoners by locking me in the cage. The cage was a small room, enclosed with bars, located in the middle of the drunk tank. There was nothing in the cage except a commode. There I spent the night, sitting on the floor with my head between my knees, my arms covering the top of my head, in a not too successful effort to protect myself from flying objects that were thrown by the other prisoners when the lights went out. Some of the objects would hit the bars or miss me completely, but some made a direct hit. They threw whatever they could get their hands on, usually a spoon or a shoe. Sometimes I would let out a big yell, hoping they would let up. It only fueled their excitement, and they would howl and laugh.

The jailer was thoroughly enjoying my torment and would come in on the pretense of restoring order, only to give everyone the opportunity of re-gathering their missiles for more action when the lights went out again. It must have been four or five o'clock in the morning when they finally stopped the bombardment.

I was released at ten o'clock Sunday morning with some bruises and a few cuts. My friend from New York never spoke a word until we were a block away from the jail. Then we both looked at each other and started to laugh, we couldn't stop. From that moment on, when we saw each other on campus, the laughter would began all over again. I never heard from my friend after those college days, but I'll bet he has entertained, and fascinated, a few New Yorker's with that story.

The speaker finally finished, and it was time to receive what we came there for. When President Derryberry called my name, and I walked across the stage to get my diploma, it was an exhilarating moment. I felt that I had finally accomplished something. A simple certificate that he placed in my hand had put me into another place in society. Oddly enough, a segment of society against which I had always rebelled. He shook my hand and congratulated me as he handed me my diploma.

When I left college, I knew that I wouldn't be satisfied with a corporate position, working certain hours on a daily and weekly basis, accumulating retirement, and vacationing two weeks a year. Even though that was far beyond any life style I had anticipated, I was already thinking of more challenging ideas.

I had a college degree and a family.

I was ready for my fifth life.

Element
5

Goat Hill

The Alabama State Capitol is located on a hill east of downtown Montgomery where goats used to graze. The hill is still referred to as "Goat Hill". I wonder if it kept its name because of the goats, or because of the human occupants?

George Corley Wallace was elected Governor of Alabama in the early 1960's on a platform of segregation today, segregation tomorrow, segregation forever. He was known as the "Fightin Little Judge", when he first ran, because he was a Circuit Judge from Barbour County and a former Golden Glove boxing champion. He was one of the most powerful Governors in the history of Alabama.

I was never an ally of George Wallace, even though I served eight years in the Legislature while he was Governor. My Mother, whose maiden name was Wallace, was the Governor's second cousin, which made Wallace and I distant relatives; but that is about as close as we got during my legislative years. I liked him personally, but politically we were enemies.

I had been elected to the Alabama House of Representatives in 1970, and I didn't know much about State Government, nor the issues. I ran against a system of rules that allowed the Governor, who was apart of the Executive Branch of Government, to organize and control the House of Representatives, which is apart of the Legislative Branch. I must have hammered that theme thousands of times during the campaign, so often, in fact, that I became identified as a political reformer who would "rock the boat". A theme which apparently gained momentum during the campaign. An "outsider" and a "reformer" combined, turned out to be a successful combination.

WON'T BARGAIN AWAY PRINCIPLE
...Bill King vows in Senate kickoff speech

Vows to 'rock boat' if elected to Senate

by Vickie Davis,
News staff writer

Vowing to help keep special interest

care if the people in Morgan Cou
want to consolidate their offices,"
said, emphasizing the need for h
rule provisions.
King told the group that house

The Huntsville News

Immediately after the primary election, Wallace called our delegation to Montgomery to let us know, among other things, who was in charge. Our delegation consisted of six legislators, four in the House, and two in the Senate.

I got lost trying to get to the Capitol for the meeting. So my first encounter with the Governor started on a negative note, because I was the last member of my delegation to arrive and fifteen minutes late at that.

The Governor's Executive Secretary invited us into the Governor's office acknowledging, while looking directly at me, that the "late member" had finally arrived.

Wallace had already been Governor for two terms, and his first wife Lurleen, one term, so by the time I met with him, I knew all about his policies and philosophy.　　But this was my first direct personal encounter, and I was intimidated.

He sat in a huge leather chair, that dwarfed him, at the head of a massive mahogany table with eight large chairs, four on each side of the table. He shook hands with each of us, as we lined up at his chair, and invited us to sit down. I found a seat at the end of the table to his left side, slumping slightly into it to avoid any attention. I listened for the major part of an hour, while he did the talking, with the support of most of our delegation.

One of his concerns was a black Dentist from Huntsville, who was running against him in the November General Election. He made a point of letting us know, that since we represented that area, that we needed to help him because, as he put it, "Nigra's will vote only for a Nigra, but white folks, especially in a liberal city like Huntsville, would sometimes vote for a Nigra."

I was offended with his use of the term "Nigra", and when he began talking about how he was going to organize the Legislature, I became annoyed. He said he hadn't made a decision yet, as to whom he wanted to be the Speaker of the House. At that moment, I knew that I had to take issue with him, or start my political career as a hypocrite, since the theme of my campaign had focused on the separation of powers doctrine.

I sucked in my breath, and with all the courage I could muster, I raised my hand, and got his attention.

He kept his eye glasses on the table, because he used them to see at distances, and he picked them up and held them to his nose as he cut his eyes to me and said, "What is it". I cleared my throat, feeling the weight of silence in the room and the eyes of all my colleagues glued to me, and I said, "Governor, with all due respect to you sir, I don't think you should be organizing the Legislature. I believe we are a separate branch of government, and in order to maintain that separation of powers, the Legislature should organize itself without any involvement from the Governor's Office".

You could have heard the proverbial "pin drop". He left me hanging there for what seemed to be minutes, then still peering at me through those glasses perched on the end of his nose, he asked me to move up next to him, claiming he could not hear very good. I moved up to the seat to his immediate left. He pulled my chair over against his, as I sat down. He then, still peering through the glasses, said "Now what was it that you said Mr......? I said, "King, Bill King", "Well Mr. King", he said, "I have a hearing problem, and you were speaking a little low, could you repeat what you said?" I could feel my face flush as I pulled myself together, and repeated it verbatim. Again he studied my face, knowing I was uncomfortable, suddenly he chuckled and said, "You know when I was first elected to the Legislature, I ran as an independent thinker too".

He insisted that I continue to sit there with my chair directly against his for the rest of the meeting.

I was relieved when he moved on to other legislative matters, although he would continue to spar with me by asking my opinion about every issue discussed that day.

He kept a cigar in his mouth the entire meeting, chewing on the end of it. As he accumulated pieces of the cigar in his mouth, he would spit them into a brass cuspidor on the floor which caused him to spit across my knees, since it was located on the opposite side of my chair.

The meeting ended about two hours later, and I was anxious to get out of there. As I started to leave, he caught me by the arm and asked me to stay for a minute.

This time he was warm and pleasant, and said my mother had written to him and asked him to look after me.

He again reiterated that he was an independent thinker as a freshman legislator, and that he wanted to work with me in the upcoming session.

That was as close as we ever got politically, during my eight years in the House and Senate. I felt insulted by his condescending manner toward me. First, he embarrassed me in the presence of my colleagues. Then, in their absence, he tried to use my mother's letter to manipulate me through implied obligation. It was easy to see why he dominated the Alabama political scene for so many decades.

As I left his office, I knew that he had drawn a line in the dust and that we were going to be in conflict. But that's what I was accustomed to.

My first election results were interesting. They reflected the backgrounds of my opponent and me. I got most of my votes, in the outlying areas, outside of the central city where former mill village and many blue collar voters lived. I also carried the black vote. My opponent got more of his support from the central city area, or the "establishment", section of the district.

I must admit that I was secretly pleased to finally overcome the Huntsville establishment.

One of my mill buddies put it best at our victory celebration when he said " I bet they won't call you lint head now!" He was referring to the times that we were run out of the downtown Central YMCA. We left, but always with a few parting comments, and a lot of laughs.

I used to wonder how they could tell, by just looking at us, that we were from the village, because we didn't have cotton lint in our hair.

I'm not sure when I decided to enter politics; although, I knew that my long standing irritation toward the establishment had a lot to do with it. I was also influenced by John Kennedy's book *Profiles In Courage,* when

I was a college student. I read it one night during my senior year. I didn't realize at the time, that I would be in the Alabama Legislature in less than a decade.

I was elected to the Alabama House of Representatives in 1970, and I didn't even know where the state capitol building was located. I knew it was in Montgomery, but I didn't know where. So on my initial visit, after my election, I had to stop at a service station, just outside of Montgomery, to get directions to the capitol.

My election to the House was won with very little financial contributions from anyone. It was mostly a lot of hard physical work throughout the district. My opponent spent most of his time around the Central City Area, in downtown Huntsville, where the establishment frequents. He was a good man. He had practiced law on the courthouse square for twenty-five years. Most of my time was spent near the factory gates and in little cafe's in the outlying part of the district. I enjoyed the hand-to-hand campaigning, and direct contact with the voters.

My four years in the House were almost uneventful. The control that Wallace's "hand picked" speaker had in the house, together with the house rules designed to allow him to control the legislative process, made it virtually impossible for change to occur.

Most of the legislation, that I proposed, never got out of committee. The speaker would rarely recognize me when I tried to challenge the process. So I used the House experience to get myself prepared for the Senate, because I knew things would be different if I could win the senate election.

I learned a lot about Alabama politics during my freshman year in the House. I listened to the political stories told by some of the Legislative members, who had served even before George Wallace. Most of these "veterans" stayed at an old downtown Montgomery hotel, named appropriately, *The Jefferson Davis Hotel*. They always frequented the hotel bar after the Legislature adjourned for the day. Many of my freshmen colleagues and I would go there, to listen to their stories, after the liquor started flowing.

One of the their favorite stories happened during the term of a colorful Alabama Governor named, James Folsom, Sr., affectionately known as "Big Jim" or "Kissin Jim". The story, as told to us, would get very animated, and probably exaggerated, because of their gullible audience. According to the story, "Big Jim" was on his way to South Alabama to name a bridge after a local Legislator, who was instrumental in getting the new bridge funded.

He was late leaving Montgomery in his chauffeur-driven limousine, recuperating from a party the night before.

He must have been in a gregarious mood, because he instructed his limo driver to stop on the highway and pick up a hitch-hiker. The hitch-hiker and Big Jim became fast friends, especially after the Governor opened a quart of whiskey.

By the time Big Jim and friend got to the dedication location, about two hours late and quite inebriated, most of the people had left. But the local legislator did his best to keep some of the crowd there, especially the newspaper reporters.

It seems that the hitch-hiker and Big Jim had become so close, during the booze sharing trip, that the Governor decided to name the bridge after the hitch-hiker, rather than the local legislator.

When Big Jim broke the news to the local Legislator, he was devastated, but the Governor smoothed it over by telling him that he would have many opportunities to have public structures named for him, but OLE..., the hitch-hiker, would never have anything named for him, so he did it. The bridge still carries the name of the hitch-hiker to this day.

I also enjoyed the story about a Legislative Committee in the House debating the evils of legalizing liquor in a south Alabama town, when the most vocal opponent, while ranting and raving about the poisonous evil of alcohol, pulled off his coat to lay it in his chair, and a half pint of bourbon fell to the floor.

The first legislative session, following my election to the House, put me, once again, on familiar turf; the outside. I became aligned with a small group of reformers who unsuccessfully opposed the house rules, which provided for a continuation of the old system. However, this same small group was successful in rewriting the Governor's budget in an all night marathon, and offered the substitute in lieu of the Governor's proposed budget.

The substitute budget was not passed, but neither was the Governor's. This maneuver resulted in the Legislative Session ending without adopting a state budget. It was the first time in the history of the state.

Most of us were freshmen legislators, and our adrenaline was surging so much after we forced an adjournment without a budget, that we all decided to go out to a small lounge just outside of Montgomery to cool down.

After many hours of "cooling", A group of female dancers, at the request of the lounge owner, came to the club to perform for the Legislators. They were, of course, strippers working on the cheering crowd with their bumps and grinds.

One of the dancer's billed as "Cherokee", was performing when I decided to go outside for air to regain my balance. My head was spinning, and I was beginning to feel sick. The stage was located just beside the exit door, as I unsteadily made my way toward it, and before I realized what was happening, the totally naked dancer, jumped astride my back. The impact threw me further off balance, and we both went sprawling ignominiously into the parking lot. The lot was covered with beer bottle caps. I felt absurd, and to this day, some of my former colleagues still relish reminding me, of the "naked Indian" incident, after all these years.

For someone who knew little about state government, by the time I had completed my term in the House, I knew the system, and used it as often as possible to protect my backside.

What a change after my election to the Senate. I knew that I could stop the entire process, if I needed to, and after being "run over", by the Wallace "machinery", for four years in the House, I was ready for the Senate battleground.

The unlimited debate rule in the Senate, called the "Filibuster," was a rule that I often used to convey my position on issues.

By the time I was elected to the Alabama Senate in 1974, I was beginning to feel that I was as good as anyone else. I started to believe what

George Wallace used to say about people in Alabama being as "refined and cultured" as anybody else. Now people referred to me as "Senator King," and I think my ego was beginning to expand, often faster than it should have, resulting sometimes in embarrassing deflation. This was something Kathrin warned me about many times.

I saw Kathrin often during my legislative days. She kept newspaper clippings, that her friends would give her, about my political activities. They were glued up on her walls for her customers to see.

She began to look a little worn after all those difficult years. I noticed that she didn't have the control of her feelings that she once had, because she would choke-up sometimes when I left, something I never saw her do before. She seemed to be trying to make it easy on me to get beyond her, by saying that she had done all she could for me and that I needed to move on. But I knew that this was her way of protecting herself, because her pain was obvious. She thought that I was visiting her out of obligation, rather than love.

The circumstances surrounding my first legislative session in the Senate was nearly as absurd as the House opening session. It was the first day of the Session in February, 1979. I was late, so I hurriedly threw some clothes together and left for Montgomery.

On the way , I received a call from my office that the Lt. Governor wanted to meet with me prior to convening the session. I was excited about meeting with him because I knew that I was going to be offered an appointment to Chair the Senate Constitution and Elections Committee.

This committee would be responsible for most of the Legislative and Constitutional reforms, which was an area in which I was particularly interested. I had won the election on a platform of similar reform issues.

My quick departure from Huntsville caused me to forget a few incidentals, including my shaving kit. After registering at the hotel, (as a matter of fact, the very hotel that I would later own when I became a developer), I rushed to the nearest convenience store to pick up a few things enroute to the Capitol.

Pulling my car onto the parking lot, and thinking only of getting to the session as soon as possible, I failed to notice that ice still covered the shaded area.

As I opened the car door, and jumped onto the ice, my feet slid out from under me, and I started to fall backwards. I automatically put my left arm back and behind my body, frantically trying to break the fall. It caught my full weight as I hit the ice. At that moment, I heard the nauseating sound that I recognized from previous injuries. I had dislocated my shoulder again.

Having experienced this injury twice before, I knew that I had to get the bone back into the socket before the swelling got too severe.

I struggled to my feet and entered the convenience store. The fall had already gotten the clerk's attention, and I asked him to pull my arm away from my shoulder so that it would snap back into the socket. He was reluctant. Being an Iranian, he could barely speak English, and had trouble understanding what I was saying. I then noticed a small grocery cart, and I asked him to hold the cart in place so that I could grasp the handle with my left hand and pull backwards, hoping that it would allow the bone to slip into the socket. He was understandably not inclined to do it.

The pain was beginning to make me feel nauseous and dizzy, so I decided to try to get to a hospital, which was enroute to the Capitol. I asked the store clerk to close my car door so that I could drive to the Emergency Room. He did.

As my "luck" continued, the Emergency Room had an intern on duty who apparently had no experience with dislocated shoulders. He directed me to lie down on a small cot, and then he began to crank my arm around in a clock-wise motion. I wondered if I could remain conscious. Each time he cranked my arm, excruciating pain shot through me, causing my entire body to rise off the cot. After a few unsuccessful attempts, he decided to call for support. His supporter turned out to be a huge hospital orderly. He must have been six and a half feet tall and probably weighed 250 pounds. He wrapped a sheet around my chest and twisted the ends until it was very tight. He then slipped off his shoe and placed his bare foot against my rib cage. Grimly bracing himself, he said in an unwavering voice, "Go ahead Doc, he won't move this time". He was right, and again I heard that sickening sound my shoulder makes when the bone snaps back into the socket.

Bum shoulder doesn't stop senator

A dislocated shoulder didn't keep state Sen. Bill King of Huntsville from the opening session of the 1977 Legislature. As he arrived at the Capitol, he stepped out of his car and slipped on ice which remained from the recent snow. He was treated at a hospital and appeared only 26 minutes late for the session. Sen. Pat Vacca of Birmingham offers condolences.

Birmingham Post Herald, February 2, 1977

I was a half hour late for the roll call on my first day in the Senate. My arm and shoulder were in a sling, and my body was throbbing with pain.

I stuffed the bills I had prepared for introduction in my sling, and when my district number was announced, I went down to the floor to introduce my bills.

This was not my only unusual experience during my term in the senate. A tree fell on my car during my participation in a filibuster.

I had been talking for about ten hours trying to defeat a bill that would allow increased truck weights and tandem trailers on the highways. It was an unsuccessful effort but a memorable one.

While I was on the floor, standing at the microphone, a tremendous thunderstorm erupted. The lights were flickering, and the Capitol Rotunda was vibrating from the thunder and lightning. The Lt.

Governor, who was clearly favorable to the Legislation, told me after a cracking thunderbolt that "The Lord" was speaking to me and wanted me to sit down and allow a vote on the measure.

The Montgomery Advertiser, April 13, 1977

As I advised him that my time was not yet up, one of the Capitol guards came in the back door of the Senate Chambers, clad in raincoat, cap, and was soaking wet. He motioned for someone to get my attention. I yielded the microphone to one of my colleagues who agreed not to yield until I returned.

The guard began shaking his head, as I walked toward him in the back. He apologetically told me that the storm had blown a tree over in the parking area, and that the tree landed directly on the top of my car.

My side lost the debate, but so did the people of Alabama, because the increased Truck Weight Bill has caused many deaths on the Alabama highways.

The Truck Weight Bill was a symptom of a diseased state government, controlled by special interest groups and politicians with little interest in reforming the system.

The National Council of State Government had just released a scathing report that ranked Alabama at the bottom of the fifty states. The report said the legislative process was the most ineffective in the nation. It cited the outdated and cumbersome constitution and Bi-annual sessions of the legislature as prime factors. Other contributing factors was the maze of state departments and agencies with ineffective evaluation and control systems, and the special interest control of the legislative process.

The Birmingham News, June 27, 1975

The release of the report shocked many members of the legislature, and brought on some critical response on the floor of both the House and Senate. But most of us knew it was factual.

It provided me with my unofficial agenda during my Senate term. My first objective was a constitutional amendment requiring the legislature to meet annually.

Getting the annual sessions bill passed required me to face, head on, the sheer power of Governor Wallace's legislative strength. His senate floor leaders had communicated to me, in very clear terms, that I would be wasting my time, because they would not allow the bill to pass.

I learned a lot about legislative maneuvers and white knuckle negotiations during that session. I also learned to turn their ruthless positioning around, and place them where they had placed me so many times.

It was never completely clear to me why the Administration opposed the Annual Sessions Bill. I suspected that it was because annual meetings, and annual budgeting would result in a more enlightened legislature, which in turn would reduce the governor's control of the process, and eliminate the need for so many costly special sessions.

The governor controlled the legislature during special sessions because the antiquated constitution provided that only the Governor could call a special session, and to further assure his control, only those issues that he put in the "call" could be passed by a simple majority. Anything else brought up in a special session would require a "two-thirds" vote of both Houses.

After the Senate passed the Annual Sessions Bill, it became bogged down in the House, because Governor Wallace controlled the speaker, who in turn controlled the flow of legislation. But I held the key to a bill that Wallace desperately wanted to pass during the session. It was a constitutional amendment to allow a forty-five million dollar bond issue for improvements to the State Docks at Mobile.

The State Docks Amendment was sponsored by Sonny Callahan, now a congressman, and a friend of mine. For the first time in my political career, I held the bargaining chip.

They didn't want these two constitutional amendments to be on the ballot at the same election. The Wallace forces, and the special interests groups, including the Alabama Farm Bureau, were prepared to kill the passage of the annual sessions amendment, by funding a major media campaign against it. If both measures were on the same ballot, they feared a major campaign against it could kill both issues and they wanted the forty-five million dollars for the state docks too much to risk it.

Callahan had carefully amended the bill in the House, to set the annual sessions vote in October, so that it would not be on the same ballot as the state dock amendment.

In the House-Senate Conference Committee meeting dealing with both issues, the tension was heavy. Both were stalled, and the Administration was desperate. As Chairman of the Senate Constitutions and Elections Committee, the destiny of the State Docks Amendment was in my hands. We needed a compromise and they knew it. I agreed to bring the bond issue out of committee on one condition; that both issues would be on the same ballot.

After a few tense moments, and a hushed conference with senators from Mobile, Callahan reluctantly agreed to go along with the proposal. The Annual Sessions and the State Docks Amendments were both approved by the voters on the same ballot.

Back during the first special session

, Sen. King and Rep. **Sonny Callahan of Mobile ran head-on over two important bills - the annual sessions act and the State Docks bond issue.**

King wanted the vote on annual sessions to come on the same day as the vote on the docks bond issue. Callahan had amended the bill to get the annual sessions vote in October. He felt the annual sessions bill on the same ticket would cause defeat of the docks bill.

In a conference committee, King give Callahan a choice. Allow the annual sessions election to be on the same ballot, support for the docks bond issue would help pass annual sessions. Callahan agreed to go along with King's proposal.

Today both of the veteran legislators, and the majority of the voters, are happy with the decision. They picked a winner in both races.

June 13, 1975, Huntsville News

The success, of the Annual Sessions Bill, encouraged me to become even more aggressive, so I tackled the inefficient organization of Alabama Government. I proposed a realignment of state departments and commissions in a Reorganization Bill, which brought the Wallace Administration forces down on me again.

Wallace-King fight brewing over state reorganization plan

Huntsville News, April 1977

When the Governor's floor leaders took the floor in the Senate, and began a blistering attack on my efforts, I realized that I had touched a sensitive nerve.

Sen. King comes out swinging for proposal

...MONTGOMERY (AP) - State Sen. Bill King of Huntsville, stinging from the slap the administration gave his government reorganization plan last week, isn't ready to turn the other cheek.

He came out swinging Tuesday when Gov. George C. Wallace's proposal to reorganize state government came up for consideration in the Alabama Senate.

When the round ended, he had won a public apology from Wallace's chief floor leader, Sen. Dudley Perry of Tuskegee, for a statement released by the governor's office last Friday.

April 13, 1977, Daily Mountain Eagle

In a sense, I was violating my own convictions, with respect to the separation of powers. I had consistently opposed attempts, by the Executive Branch, to interfere with legislative issues, yet my bill would, if passed, reorganize the structure of state government, a traditional responsibility of the Executive Branch.

A major floor fight pursued in the Senate that lasted for three weeks. A filibuster tied the session up for much of that time.

I knew I was beginning to make progress when the Wallace floor leaders apologized for the criticism and began to talk about compromise. We passed the first reorganization of Alabama State Government in the State's history.

Montgomery Advertiser

Senator Receives Apology
For Reorganization Attack

By BOB LOWRY
Advertiser Staff Writer

State Sen. Bill King of Huntsville fired a volley back Tuesday at the Wallace Administration which had harshly criticized his alternate plan for state government reorganization last week.

And King won a public apology on the floor of the Alabama Senate from Gov. George C. Wallace's chief floor leader, Sen. Dudley Perry of Tuskegee.

Perry told King he was "somewhat offended myself" by the statement which was released last Friday by Wallace's office and attributed only to the "administration."

"I personally apologize to you," said Perry. "That statement should have been attributed to the governor's office and not the governor himself." He added

up last Thursday and King attempted to substitute the bill with a plan of his own. So far the Senate has adopted neither plan.

On Friday, the statement from Wallace's office described King's bill as a "smokescreen" and a reshuffling, not a reorganization of state agencies. It also accused King of attempting to "gut" the reorganization effort.

King said Tuesday that the statement was "incredible," adding, "I find it hard to believe that the governor himself would issue such a statement as the one released Friday, especially since I tried for a week to convey my concerns with the reorganization bill as introduced.

Wallace's plan would combine the more than 200 state agencies under 15 new departments, while King's would reduce it down to six major depart-

state government," which he said are evaluation, performance and accountability, control and management of higher education, restrictions on state employment, reduction in operating costs and duplication.

"In Alabama we must face three alternatives with respect to state government: increase revenue, reduce services or the one which I like is simply getting more effectiveness and efficiency with existing resources," said King.

He gave a point-by-point defense Tuesday of the points raised in the Wallace statement last week.

"It is unfortunate when an issue as important as reorganization cannot be discussed from a number of alternatives among public officials without launching attacks," he said.

"Certainly both bills can stand con-

My agenda had two major issues left to pursue; the outdated constitution, and the budgeting process.

I prepared a bill, called "The Budget Management Act." The bill would require state government department heads to establish goals and objectives for their departments, submit them to the state legislature, and be evaluated annually on the cost effectiveness of the operations.

This bill stirred up the Administration almost as much as the Reorganization Bill. The budgeting process, required by the legislation, would require sound goals and objectives, and a monitoring system not familiar to most of the department heads in state government. It was structured to focus attention on those appointed for political reason, rather than management skills.

The bill passed, in spite of the Administrations opposition. To the governor's credit, he didn't attempt to veto it, and it became law in 1976. Unfortunately IT WAS NEVER IMPLEMENTED, even though it is the law.

My legislative career, as a non-lawyer, also made my life interesting, because I was the only non-lawyer on the Senate Judiciary Committee. On most committee votes, I voted in opposition to lawyers interest. The chairman, good naturedly, would announce the vote before it was taken by saying, "Nine yeas and one nay", "Senator King votes, no". He was usually right.

However, I did manage to win a few on the Judiciary Committee. One successful attempt allowed persons, who could not read, to serve on juries.

Another successful one allowed blacks to serve on the State Pardon-Parole Board. It was inconceivable, that in the history of the State of Alabama, no blacks had ever served on the State Pardon-Parole Board until that bill passed.

Sen. King to ask Expansion of Pardons and Parole Board

"Since blacks are represented in the Alabama state prison population," King said, "it is both logical and just that such representation should also be reflected in the (board's) membership"

March 18, 1977, The Huntsville Times

While I did, and do, have many lawyers as friends, I also had many battles with lawyer interests and the State Bar Association.

As in my business career, I won some and lost some. One of my most disappointing efforts was my attempts to revise Alabama's outdated constitution. Sadly, that same outdated 1901 constitution is still in existence at this writing, 99 years after it was written, with more than 600 amendments.

King: State Government in Crisis

State Sen. Bill King of Huntsville, who said he plans to run for lieutenant governor next year, said there is a crisis in Alabama government..."I don't say it is any reflection of the chief executive, it lies in Alabama government. We haven't taken the responsibility to look five or 10 years ahead."..."The Alabama constitution is outdated not because it's old, but because it doesn't deal with today's problems."

He proposed a solution to the problems--a new constitution.

June 24, 1977, Birmingham Post-Herald

While most of my senate activity was opposed by the Administration, I attempted to keep my communications with Governor Wallace open and amicable.

During one amusing event, I had been selected by the State Conservation Commission as the "Conservationist of The Year." Governor Wallace was the Ex-officio' Chairman of the commission, and had to present me with the trophy, which was a black bear, with a plaque on its base.

When he presented me with the trophy he whispered, "Bill, you're a Bear!" I knew that he was sensitive about his age and that he had another birthday the week before the ceremony. I whispered back, "congratulations on another birthday, Governor". We both chuckled.

While I was comfortable with my position on most of the battles with the Administration, there were times when I struggled with my conscience and my personal feelings, when they were at odds with the people I represented. I sometimes questioned the democratic principle of representative government. Should I vote my personal convictions or those of my constituents, when they differed.

During my eight years as an elected official, I only regret casting one vote. It had to do with the equal rights amendment for women. It was a U. S. Constitutional Amendment which, when ratified by thirty-six state legislatures, would become apart of the U.S. Constitution.

The issue was hotly debated in the media. Most of the conservative women groups were opposed to it, while the National Association for Women was favorable. Organizations, of conservative women's groups, argued that it would jeopardize housewives' position, and women in general, with respect to custody law and divorce settlements. Professional women groups argued that it was merely equalizing women, with respect to men in terms of equal opportunity and pay.

I struggled with this issue, because I was personally in favor of it. But a newspaper survey, which I commissioned for constituents opinions, showed that 60 percent of my Senate district was opposed to the amendment.

This was the beginning of an agonizing internal battle for me. Should I vote my feelings, taking the position that voters elected me, to evaluate the issues and decide what was best for them? Or should I be a vehicle for their views, and vote against the issue, disregarding my own personal feelings? I am sure that every elected official has had to face this dilemma. I chose the safe way politically and voted with my constituents and against my own conviction. This is one vote I wish I could recast.

I must admit that I rationalized my vote because I was going to run for Lt. Governor, and I knew that in Alabama, my vote in opposition was more favorable for the majority of the voters. This is an example of compromising for political expediency. I also knew that the amendment would not be ratified by the Alabama Legislature. Actually, few members of the Senate thought the issue would ever get to the floor for a vote because of the controversy surrounding the issue.

The real reason that it came up for a vote was to force the potential statewide candidates to take a position on the issue for campaign purposes.

I was already dealing with the duplicity required to continue to progress in politics. This was the issue that caused me to go to the depth of my conscience, and realize what was happening to me.

Leadership In Senate Blasted by Sen. King

By Guy Hollis, Times Staff Writer...Montgomery

"The special interest groups have the funds to put into election campaigns," said King, "and consequently they get favorable treatment from the legislature."

King said that a senator has two choices in fighting what he termed the "system."

"I can fight the system and perhaps live better with myself and my conscience," said King. "If I do that, then anything I get passed will be held to a minimum."

"on the other hand, I can come in and vote with them and perhaps get a few bills passed."

The Huntsville Times

The most difficult part of campaigning for me was fund raising. I detested having to ask for contributions ,because I felt that it implied obligation.

I remember my humiliation once, while running for Lt. Governor. A big time contributor left word at my Campaign Headquarters that he wanted to see me. So I made arrangements to get to his office at his convenience. He was a wealthy person. Not only powerful at the state level, but a rich and powerful man in the district, developing shopping centers and dealing in major real estate transactions.

When I visited his office, he seemed to be preoccupied. He briefly discussed what he thought was important, never asking me my opinion on any of his topics.

As our visit ended, and I got up to leave his office, he pointed to an envelope lying on the corner of his desk and asked me to take it. I felt awkward, because of the manner in which he did it. I picked up the envelope and opened it when I got to my car. It contained four hundred dollars in cash. He didn't use a check, because he obviously didn't want to be identified as one of my supporters, yet he wanted to obligate me by hedging his bet and purchase a "door opener", in case he needed it later. I knew that he had done the same thing with other candidates, and that it was his way of "covering his ass."

I carried the envelope back into his office and handed it to his secretary asking her to give it back to him.

"Go Get Him, I'll Hold" . . .

. . . the secretary was told, after she had explained that

Sen Bill King was on the floor of the Senate and could not be disturbed.

The early-morning caller was a wealthy Huntsville businessman who stood to save several thousand dollars annually from passage of a couple of bills relating to property taxes. The secretary offered to take a number, but he insisted on holding.

She did not know exactly how to explain the situation to King, but finally she did.

"Tell him to hold until 4 am and we might take a break," King replied.

More than slightly embarrassed, the secretary nevertheless went back upstairs and delivered the message.

Click.

May 1, 1977, The Huntsville Times

I lost the election for Lt. Governor by a few thousand votes, but I never looked back. I knew that I had accumulated enough powerful political enemies, including the trucking and strip mining companies and the Wallace machine, that winning a statewide election would be difficult, if not impossible. Kathrin knew how much stress politics was putting on me, and she was pleased that I was leaving it.

The last time I had personal contact with George Wallace was in New York City at the Democratic National Convention. The Democrats were about to nominate a southerner from Georgia to be the Democratic Nominee for the Presidency. Jimmy Carter, a former Georgia Governor and a compassionate moderate, was not only about to become the parties nominee, but he was also about to become the first, "deep south" President since Reconstruction.

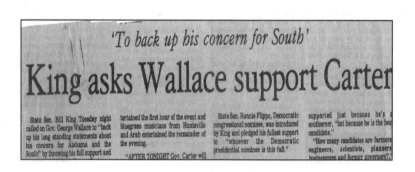

'To back up his concern for South'

King asks Wallace support Carter

State Sen. Bill King Tuesday night called on Gov. George Wallace to "back up his long standing statements about his concern for Alabama and the South" by throwing his full support and

tertained the first hour of the event and bluegrass musicians from Huntsville and Arab entertained the remainder of the evening.

"AFTER TONIGHT Gov. Carter will

State Sen. Ronnie Flippo, Democratic congressional nominee, was introduced by King and pledged his fullest support to "whoever the Democratic presidential nominee is this fall."

supported just because he's a southerner, "but because he is the best candidate."

"How many candidates are farmers, engineers, scientists, planners, businessmen and former governors?."

I was Carter's delegate from Alabama and I had no idea what I was supposed to be doing, but it didn't matter because his nomination was a foregone conclusion.

I thought about George Wallace during the Convention Preliminaries. Somehow, he always felt that he would be the first southerner from deep south to be elected President.

One of my Senate colleagues from Mobile was also in New York for the Convention, and the two of us decided to go to the hotel where Governor Wallace was staying to visit with him before the convention nominating process began.

Being Governor of Alabama, he was still the official party leader for Alabama and accorded that courtesy from national party officials.

The Wallace staff had a complete wing of the hotel, including the area from the elevator to the end of the hall, which consisted of about twelve hotel rooms and a meeting room.

Cornelia Wallace, was the Governor's wife at that time, and she was the official hostess. She met us at the hotel elevators. She was very cordial, and asked that we wait a few minutes while Wallace's aides got him ready for visitors.

I was unprepared for the shock that I got as I walked into his room. The fiery Governor from Alabama, who had taken on Federal Judges and defied a United States Attorney General over the integration of the University of Alabama was a pathetic sight. He was lying on a large bed, his head supported with two pillows, and the lower part of his body looked lifeless. His legs and feet were lying flat on the bed as if they were stuffed. I was emotionally touched by the sight.

It was difficult to view this broken body, knowing the strong vibrant man that once existed within. He had dominated Alabama Politics for two decades.

I could visualize him pounding his fist on the podium, as he drove insults down the throats of Federal Judges, while inciting the voters to take control and get the Federal Government off their backs. I could almost hear him shouting about giving the Federal Judges a "barbed wire enema". It was sobering to realize that this fragile person lying on the bed today, was the same man.

He was pale, and obviously in pain, as he strained to smile at the two of us. He thanked us for coming to see him. He focused on me for a minute and said, "Bill, I know you are a strong Carter supporter, but this would have been my nomination if I hadn't got shot!" When I smiled without verbally responding, he chuckled and said, "That's all right, Carter don't believe it either".

His spirit seemed to improve as we talked, in fact he almost seemed like his ole self as he began to make political wise-cracks about the process, and dropping some of his famous and funny one-liners.

As we prepared to leave, he said, "I know ya'll got political ambitions, and you both might make it to Governor someday". He was looking at both of us when he asked, "What are you running for Bill?" Since both of us were named Bill, we simultaneously started to respond. After yielding to my friend, I said that I was thinking about running for Lt. Governor, but that I was beginning to get a little disillusioned with politics. He said, "You'll get over that".

Ironically both my colleague and I were in the race for Lt. governor in the 1978 election. Neither of us were successful, but we have remained friends.

This was my first attendance at a national convention. I was in awe of the Celebrities. Most of the national television anchors and news people were around the convention headquarters interviewing candidates, campaign managers and others. United States Senators and Congressmen were on the floor conversing with Delegates. Movie stars and entertainers were plentiful. I sat with Larry Gatlin, of the Gatlin Brothers Band, at the delegate dinner.

When I ended my senate term, I was ready to move on, eight years in the legislature was about as much as I could handle.

The duplicity, required in public office, discouraged me, especially after an incident involving one of my constituents during the latter part of my senate term.

It happened on a hot Saturday while I was riding my motorcycle, as I often did on weekends. I stopped at a local service station to get gas. When I took my helmet off, to cool my head, a lady in the car at the next pump recognized me. She seemed indignant and said, "If I had known you rode one of those things, I would never have voted for you". She drove off before I could recover. That short, but direct, message stayed with me for the weekend. I had tried to be more discreet with my private activities, yet I resented the inference that riding a motorcycle somehow made me an undesirable public official.

I spent the rest of the day enjoying the cool spring air in the mountains and valleys of North Alabama on my motorcycle, while I struggled with a decision to seek the Office of Lt. Governor.

Willie Nelson was appropriately singing, *Unclouded Day* into my helmet ear phones as I weaved in and out of the curves coming down Monte Sano mountain. I decided not to let the woman at the gas station ruin my day, besides she probably didn't vote for me anyway. But she did cause me to revisit my decision-making process two years earlier, when I had decided to seek the Senate seat.

The Senate election was much more difficult than the House for a number of reasons. One was that the area was so much larger than the House District. Another was my opponent. He was well known, and politically popular. He had already served two terms in the House, and he was chairman of our delegation. Being chairman gave him much more exposure, and allowed him to speak, on many occasions, for the entire delegation.

He was a member of the Huntsville Country Club, and a bonefide member of the establishment. I knew from the beginning that he would get the support from the same people that opposed me in the House Election and, for some reason, the possibility of taking them on again excited me.

Gradually, without being consciously aware of it, I was becoming a part of the Huntsville establishment. After my election to the Senate, I lived in an exclusive historical preservation district in an elegant old house that was built in 1889. It was formerly the home of the county's only circuit judge in the early 1900's. I was an active member of the Rotary Club, and I knew all of the business and political leaders in the area. In fact, my office was located only a block away from the central YMCA, where much of the damage to my self-esteem originated. My initial resentment had faded somewhat, and my life had changed considerably. I began to put my early years in the background, and block completely some painful experiences.

King
'In Return, I Hope They Only Expect The Philosophy of Government I Have'
By PETER COBUN, Times Staff Writer

'Often Bill King sits in the steam room at the Central YMCA downtown, and remembers those days of growing up in Huntsville when he was told that "lintheads" such as he had their own "Y".
...But Bill King eventually escaped the village and its class prejudice,...he insists he harbors no resentment of those earlier times.'

June 26, 1977, The Huntsville Times

I turned my motorcycle around, headed back over the mountain, down the valley, and across the river to Kathrin's place. She was preparing for a typical Saturday night in her lounge, washing and cleaning off the screened back porch. She still had the newspaper clippings of my Senate election on her kitchen wall. They were turning yellow after two years. She was a little cool, because I hadn't visited her in almost a month. I told her about the woman at the gas station, and she was amused. She said some white people still hadn't learned to see beyond the surface, and that I should understand that by now. She was right, and my burden became somewhat less.

I really got her attention when I asked her what she thought about my running for Lt. Governor at the next election. She looked, not at me, but into me and asked why. I struggled to answer her, but the truth was that I didn't know, and I wasn't prepared to answer. I finally came out with a pitiful response about my commitment to better government, but she wasn't buying it.

She was seeing me exposed, as she had so many times before. She said "You don't really know why, and if you work at it long enough, you will come up with a good answer", then, in her very biased opinion, she added, "But you will do a good job so just get on with it. I'll talk to Hobo, Clarence, all their friends, and work the church and the black community for you. So don't get yourself killed before the election gets here".

The ride back was beautiful, Willie was now singing, *On The Road Again*, and I knew what I was going to do. As I got close to town, I turned off to ride through the mill village and see if I could see my long time friend, "Floyd the Barber".

Floyd Hardin's shop was now located in an old converted mill house. It was like a museum for the Dallas mill village and Rison School. The walls were covered with pictures of people who grew up in the village. I could walk around the shop and see my picture, and those of my friends, their brothers, sisters, mothers, and fathers. Our high school football team group picture was on the wall by Floyd's chair, with my friends and me looking very young and trying to look mean.

When I wheeled into the parking lot, I could see Floyd sitting in the swing on the porch of the shop. He saw me take off my helmet and laughed, shook his head ,and said, "Come on up and cool off."

I told him what I was thinking and he said, "You know you will get the support of the mill village folks and all of their relatives, but a statewide race is a lot different from a local election." How right he was. As I left the barber shop, I again realized how fortunate I had been with my early years in the mill village, and with Kathrin, and I was ashamed for trying to separate myself from this essential part of my being years earlier. I rode through the village thinking about the good times that I had running up and down the back alleys. The motorcycle ride was clearing my thinking, and helping me to arrive at a decision with respect to the election, which was about two years away.

I rode down Fifth Street and past the old location of the poolroom, where I spent much of my youth, and thought about the five lifetimes I had already lived.

Part II

Oval Office

As I waited outside the Oval office in July, 1977 for my appointment with the President, many things ran through my mind. I was struck by the fact that two hundred and one years ago, almost to the day, this country declared it's independence, and fought a war to maintain it. I felt awed to be sitting in the building where every President of the United States, with the exception of George Washington, had lived.

Jim Free, Carter's campaign coordinator, was talking to me while we waited for the President. He said that I was there because President Carter felt that I had earned a Presidential appointment. As Carter's Alabama Campaign Chairman, we had brought Alabama into the winning column. This was considered significant, since Alabama had been in the Republican category for the previous three presidential elections.

I liked President Carter, I thought he was a good and decent man, who was sincerely dedicated to his role as a public official. He was committed to being the best President he could be. Unfortunately, circumstances beyond his control cost him the election for a second term; but he has never varied from his deep commitment to the American people.

As we waited, my mind drifted back to the early years of my life living in the mill village, and attending Rison School. I thought of the pool-

room, where I spent most of my time when I was not in school, and where
I spent a lot of the time when I should have been in school. The poolroom
was the home away from home for most of the village boys. Most of my
"street learning" came from listening to the older guys talking about girls,
cars, and sex. I wondered what their reaction would be if they knew I was
in the President's office.

The clack of pool balls faded slowly from my mind, and I returned
to the Oval Office. I was struck by the thought of the major decisions that
had been initiated within these walls; Abraham Lincoln and the
Emancipation Proclamation; Franklin Roosevelt's decision to enter World
War II; Harry Truman's decision to drop the Atomic Bomb on Japan; and
John F. Kennedy's decision to put a man on the moon. The more I
thought about these events, the more insignificant I felt. I was here to be
appointed, by the President, to The Commission on Intergovernmental
Relations, hardly an event of national significance. Actually, few people
had ever heard of the Commission, but to me it was significant.

My thoughts wondered back, even farther past the poolroom days,
to my grandfather and grandmother. They had come to Huntsville from
a small rural town in North Alabama named "Paint Rock", bringing with
them a house full of children consisting of my mother, her two sisters, and
five brothers.

The mill management allowed them to live in an old, converted, two story school building, that had about eight rooms and a kitchen, provided they would keep as boarders, mill workers who had no place to live. My grandfather worked as a school janitor and my grandmother operated the boarding house. She cleaned, and cooked three meals a day, for the boarders and her extended family, which included, in addition to her own children, my father, my sister, and me.

My grandfather could not read or write, but he and my grandmother worked hard to provide their eight children with the education they themselves never had. I could still see the old boarding house. It was a red brick building facing to the south. The front entrance had a huge door, which opened into the main room. The center structure was octagon shaped with two stories. There was an east and a west wing with three rooms each on one level. The wings also had outside entrances and access inside to the center structure. My mother, father, sister, and I lived in the west wing. The boarders and my uncles lived upstairs, and my grandparents lived in the east wing with my mother's youngest sister.

The main room was large with an iron spiral stairway in the center of the room. The furnishings were sparse; they included an old worn divan, two rocking chairs, and a few straight back chairs. All of the chairs had woven bamboo seats.

One of the rocking chairs, near the door to the east wing, was the one my mother and grandmother used to rock me to sleep. It had a rhythmic squeak, as it rocked back and forth, that made me sleepy, even when someone else was rocking in it.

The building was used as the mill village's first school for the first, second, and third grades, before being converted into a boarding house. My stepfather had attended school there when he was in the third grade.

There were no newspapers or radios at the boarding house and television wasn't available, but everyone there knew that Franklin D. Roosevelt was the President. I wondered how my grandparents would feel if they knew I was meeting today with the President of the United States.

What a contrast, I thought, looking at the ornate foyer of the Oval Office and comparing it to the drab, worn main room of the boarding house.

When I was three my family moved from the boarding house to a small house in the lower mill village area, where I lived until my father died.

As I reminisced, I wondered how many people worked in the White House kitchen and how the meals were served to the First Family. I could vaguely recall those big meals that my grandmother prepared and served to the boarders and her family around a huge dinner table. I enjoyed eating with the boarders, they always seemed jolly. During the first three years of my life I shared every meal with a dozen people.

My thoughts drifted again to the past. The things which flashed across my mind this time were not about the boarding house, but about Kathrin and the good times I used to have in the summer at her place. I was eager to tell her about my visit with the President. I remembered how proud she was when I won my first election to the Alabama House of Representatives in 1970, and even more when I was elected to the State Senate in 1974. She was excited about my political activities, but she refused to participate openly. She had always felt that our public association would be a risk to both of us. The twisted public mind could be unforgiving, and possibly vicious, if they knew of the maternal relationship between a black woman and a white boy.

The combination of the rough and tumble mill village years, coupled with Kathrin's wisdom and influence, really did more to keep my feet firmly on the ground than all my other lessons in life combined.

Bits and pieces of memories of Kathrin swam to the surface of my mind, like leaves swirling in the eddies of the creek a couple of miles behind Kathrin's house.

There are moments, and places in the south, where time seems to stand still and only the present exists. I experienced such moments in those creek bank afternoons.

I found myself comparing Jimmy Carter's "born again", Christian faith to Kathrin's. I remembered when she and her sister would take me to those African American church meetings in rural North Alabama. I thought about how welcomed I felt there. I remembered how awkward I felt the first time, and how that changed after the first Sunday.

Jim Free broke into my thoughts again to ask me if I was going to continue in politics, or move on to other things. At the time, I wasn't sure. I told him that if I was unsuccessful in my bid for Lt. Governor, I would possibly submerge myself in the development business, and not surface for the next four or five years. I didn't realize, at the time, how prophetic my words were.

As abruptly as he had appeared, he disappeared again, too busy to talk. He kept bouncing in and out, talking on the phone, and trying to make me comfortable, all at the same time; but I didn't mind being left alone with my thoughts.

I reflected on Jim's question about my future in the political arena. I had already been elected to the Alabama House and Senate, and there were other things that had begun to draw my interest. In addition, I wasn't sure that I could endure the duplicity that politics demanded much longer.

My musings, on the moral dilemmas of politics, led me to think about events in my early years, which had pushed me past my imagined boundaries. One of those events, still fresh in my mind after many years, was the first time that I was challenged to contemplate my future. My tenth grade teacher asked our class to write down our life goals. As I pondered his question, all I could think of was getting out of high school, and getting a job. College never entered my mind, nor did it enter the minds of most of my classmates, because our responses were similar. Our influences did not extend any further than the associations we had in the classroom and in the village.

Consequently, when I was selected at sixteen to live in France as an exchange student, I was perplexed. My boundaries were being tested. I had reservations about my abilities to adjust to such a change. I had rarely been out of Alabama.

The thought of spending a year in Europe was both intimidating and exciting. I did, however, choose to go.

My thoughts of the past dissipated when Jim Free approached to introduce me to Hamilton Jordan, President Carter's Press Secretary. Hamilton was very cordial, but obviously to busy to chat. He said that the

White House photographers would be at our meeting for a photo session. I wondered if the picture would appear in my local newspaper. It did. Hamilton departed, and Jim Free apologized because he had to leave again for a few minutes.

Presidential Appointment, White House Oval Office

I was relieved, and went back into another anxious trance. This time I thought about my father, Ben King. I knew very little about him. I remember my mother telling me that the day I was born, he said I would be President. Probably, most father's say something boastful like that when their first son is born. I think I did.

He was a strange, shy, man, who rarely talked. He grew up in a sharecropper shack in Lincoln, Tennessee. His mother, my grandmother, was a Cherokee Indian with a non-smiling, leathery face. I remember that my mother would compel me to hug her when we went to visit, and it was like hugging a wooden statue; she never responded. He was very much the same, undemonstrative, and seemingly unemotional.

He had very little education, having dropped out of school after the third grade to join his brothers and sisters working in the fields. Yet he was committed to finishing high school through correspondence courses, and he worked at a little desk every night until bedtime.

He was a truck driver for his cousin's trucking business when he and my mother married. I don't remember any affection or warmth from him, but I do remember some pretty severe beatings.

One in particular was when I was four years old. It was Christmas, and I knocked my sister's tea set off a little table onto the floor. My father was determined to make me pick it up, but I refused. He then decided to whip me into submission. I was just as determined not to yield, so he beat me until my mother and grandmother left the room. Finally, I gave in, but I never cared much for him after that, and I was never comfortable around him.

When I was eight years old, he was injured in a softball game. The injury damaged his kidneys. We were too poor to afford proper medical treatment. Eventually his kidney's failed. He was sent to Vanderbilt Hospital in Nashville, on a public assistance medical program. He died there within a few months.

Everyone in the mill village, and at school lavished me with pity. It made me feel guilty, because I didn't feel any sorrow.

I wondered if President Carter had a close relationship with his children. I had met his son, Chip, during the campaign, and I liked him very much. He attended a campaign function on the lawn of my house in Huntsville. It was a political/social event for Carter, held just prior to the General Election. There were four or five hundred people, from all around the county, in attendance; legislators, judges, teachers, etc.

Chip spent the night at my house. After the guests had left, we sat in my study, with a bottle of vodka, and talked until dawn. After a while, the conversation turned to our fathers. He spoke affectionately about his.

Chip was curious about my life in the mill village. I was somewhat apologetic about my background, even though I knew that the President had little concern about a person's pedigree. I told him of my efforts to get beyond the mill village by working my way through college on the sewer line crew. He seemed amused.

Jim Free brought me back to the present again briefly when he said, "Only a couple more minutes". The "couple" of minutes turned out to be forty-five, but I really didn't mind. It was a good time for me to ponder my past, and watch the serious, but pompous, activity in the White House.

I remembered some of the political rallies for Carter in Alabama, and how we promoted him as a peanut farmer from Georgia. I still have some of those peanuts that we handed out at the rallies. They were painted white with a full smiling face, and the farmers loved them. I often wondered if those rallies were really effective, or merely an exercise for a candidate and his supporters to get together and test their speeches and evaluate opponents.

Carter, Wallace, and King

I thought about how ridiculous one rally was, during my own candidacy for the Senate. I was scheduled to speak at a rural high school, along with other candidates that included those for Judge, District Attorney, Sheriff, etc. I got there late, and had to park on the other side of a small ditch. When I got out of my car, and stretched one of my legs across the small water-filled ditch, the entire seat of my pants ripped open. It was a tan poplin suit, and my underwear was clearly visible.

Thoroughly frustrated, I rushed into the school, and slipped onto the stage, through a side door, taking my seat. I listened to the standard political rhetoric from the speakers for a while. Finally, my time in the program came and I was introduced. I had to walk to the podium holding the seat of my pants together with one hand. I first apologized to Myrtle Green, the incumbent candidate for County Probate Judge, who happened to be sitting directly behind me. Her face became crimson, and then she, good naturedly, burst out laughing. I then sheepishly explained to the audience what had happened to my pants. The story brought laughter and applause.

After the speeches were finished, the candidates began working the crowd. It was a little awkward for me, because as I shook hands with people, I had to hold the seat of my pants together with the other hand.

The embarrassing incident reaped rewards, because I was the one candidate, out of fifteen or so, that the crowd would surely remember, not because of my speech, but because of my pants. My opponent later accused me of ripping my pants on purpose.

That rally proved to be memorable for me in another way. It was an evening in which I encountered an intersection with my past. As I was making my way through the crowd, I noticed three men standing over to the side, as though they were waiting for people to clear out before approaching me. It was obvious that they were poor farmers. They had on old overalls and gray work shirts. The oldest one held a cap in his hand. I moved to them and held out my hand, the oldest one looked at the floor and said shyly, "I'm Ben's brother".

Standing there was my father's brother and his two sons, my cousins, neither of whom I had ever met. They continued to look at the floor while they talked to me, and occasionally with their hands over their mouths they would chuckle, obviously still enjoying the ripped pants episode.

I felt such an unexpected rush of warmth toward them, that I wanted to hug them, but I knew they would be uncomfortable with that much familiarity. So we just chatted for awhile, and then parted. I never saw them again, but I was genuinely touched that they had made the effort to be there.

It was finally time to see the President, as Jim Free led me into the Oval Office, I could feel my pulse accelerate. The excitement was overwhelming as President Carter met me half-way across the room, his hand outstretched, and a big smile on his face, he said, "Hi Bill, I'm sorry you had to wait". He thanked me for my support, and said he appreciated my accepting the presidential appointment. The White House photographer was entering the office, ready to take the photographs. He asked that we just continue talking, and disregard his presence. I don't remember what my response to the President was, other than "Thank you", and "I look forward to participating..." He then put his hand on my shoulder and asked how my campaign was going. It impressed me that he knew I was running for Lt. Governor. He said he could remember how difficult his first statewide campaign was, and told me not to get discouraged. He was very sincere and genuine, and we conversed for almost twenty minutes before his Executive Secretary advised him of his critical schedule.

As we parted, he expressed his concern about George Wallace's health.

Leaving the White House, I couldn't help thinking about these two powerful Southerners, and how different they were. They had been Governors of sister southern states, both had been candidates for President.

How different they were in style and philosophy. I was pleased that I had the unique experience of knowing both of them, and observing their commonalties and differences.

I served on the Commission for three years, attending my first meeting during that trip to Washington. I was duly impressed with the members, one of which was the current Secretary of the Interior, Bruce Babbit. Senator William Roth, from Delaware, who authored the Roth IRA Legislation, was also one of the Commissioners. In addition, there were other U.S. Senators, Governors, and large city Mayors among its members.

Part III

Behind the
Iron Curtain

November, 1976, Moscow, Russia, U.S.S.R. The huge jet came slowly to rest in the Russian National Airport. I was now behind the "Iron Curtain", and my adrenaline was surging.

There we would wait, for the better part of two hours, before we would even begin the customs process. I was immediately identified, by the customs agent, as a Carter Election Official. There were about thirty people on the plane. Some were State Department Officials.

We were to be there for the next fifteen days, visiting with the Russian Foreign Relations Office, and touring Industrial Communities, Lenin's Tomb, and some of the beautiful castles from the CZAR era. Most of us were laymen, and newly associated with National Politics and Government, and that's what the Russian Officials wanted. We had no set agenda; we were there to learn something of the Russian culture. My wife accompanied me, and she was nervous, not only because of being out of the country for the first time in her life, but also being completely on the other side of the planet, in a communist country.

Jimmy Carter had just won the General Election, about three weeks prior to the trip. The excursion was hastily put together, within about a two week period. We were jointly selected by the Senate Foreign Relations Committee and Carter campaign officials.

Late November in Russia is severely cold, especially in Northern Russia. Those of us from the deep south were less than adequately prepared.

Since Carter had just been elected, but had not yet assumed the Office of the Presidency, the Russian people were very curious about him. They identified with his "peanut farmer" background, but they had great distrust of American political officials.

During the two hour delay at the airport, I was straining to look out the window of the airplane. I was curious to see what the Russian people actually looked like. I could see a few men and women working around the planes, dressed with big coats and wool caps, and some handling luggage, or driving little carts.

We were given last minute instructions, by the State Department, to be very careful to adhere to the guidelines given by our Russian Guides, a warning that I disregarded, on one occasion, which nearly got me more time in Russia than I wanted.

After four grueling hours of customs, we were taken to our hotel in Moscow. I think it was the largest hotel in the world, at that time, with accommodations for six thousand people in one building.

I became friends with our initial guide. He could speak English rather well, and was fascinated with his role as our guide. He appeared to be about thirty years old. His status was equivalent to an "intern", in the U.S. State Department. I told him that my copy of Newsweek magazine, with Jimmy Carter's picture on the cover, was missing. I told him that it was in my bag when I began the customs process, but it was not there when my bags were returned. He smiled, scrugged his shoulders, and said,

"They will hold it for you until you leave".

I quickly learned, from my guide, that a common mistake that Americans make in the Soviet Union, is to refer to all of them as Russians. Actually, Russians comprised only about half of the total population. There were one hundred and four nationalities speaking one hundred and twenty different languages in the U.S.S.R.

I also learned that I needed permission to make pictures of the people, and the most important rule of all was, that I must not venture on my own, without the guides permission. These rules made my curiosity even stronger. I was naive to think that I could push the envelope, ever so slightly, without taking a lot of risk.

Our first three days in Moscow were fascinating. Our hotel, Rossiya, was located directly across from Red Square and the Kremlin.

My first day was almost a total loss. I had severe "jet lag" and my mind was numb. However, I managed the tour following a very unappetizing breakfast of fish at the hotel.

I was not accustomed to leaving my key with the hotel when I wasn't in my room, as was the Russian requirement. This routine added to my already suspicious feelings about the Soviet Union, especially after my Newsweek magazine left my bag at the airport customs office.

On each floor of the hotel, near the elevator, there was the equivalent of a hotel front desk clerk. When we left the hotel floor, we had to turn the room key over to this person, and retrieve it when we returned. Which meant they had access to our room and personal belongings while we were away, and they knew our schedules. In reality, I suppose that the same thing is true in the United States, since all hotels have master keys. The difference was that we only had a key to our room while we were in it.

Moscow was a city of pilgrimage, in 1976, just as Jerusalem, Mecca, and Rome. The difference was that the pilgrimage in Red Square consists of long lines, filing past Lenin's embalmed body, in the great Mausoleum of Red Square. We lined up for the same reason, and the process took about two hours.

My guide informed me that Napoleon was the only warrior to occupy Moscow, and only for a brief period, but that was over one hundred and fifty year's before our visit.

Moscow sums up the Russian character and destiny. It was the administrative, legislative, educational, and cultural capital of the U.S.S.R. I was fascinated being inside the great red brick walls of the Kremlin, the seat of government for most of the communist world, especially the Palace of Congresses with its immense auditorium and a seating capacity of six thousand.

My tour of the Grand Kremlin Palace was intimidating. This was the seat of the Supreme Soviet of the U.S.S.R., and the Russian Federal Soviet Republic. It was open to visitors, only on special occasions, and I was humbled to be there, to say the least.

The Spassky Tower is the finest, and most ornate, of the many bastions built to defend the main entrance of the Kremlin. There are about eighteen other towers reinforcing the red brick battlement walls of the Kremlin. We attended briefings, and cultural exchange meetings, at various locations within the Kremlin.

I was beginning to be a little more aggressive, during some of our encounters, until I was gracefully admonished by my guide that we were not here to debate the benefits of Capitalism or Communism, but to learn from each other in open forum. I needed his counseling, and I felt a little guilty, so I asked that he accompany me back to one of the Russian Officials that I had challenged to apologize. He did, and the official insisted that it was his fault. I knew it wasn't, but I was impressed with his unselfishness.

On our first "open night", we went to the old Moscow Circus, just a short distance from the hotel. Popov, the famous Russian clown, was one of the mainstays. It was the most entertaining circus that I had ever seen. I was equally amused at the reaction of the Russian people. Both adults and children were so involved in the performances, that they were as entertaining as the performers. I have never seen a performance so thoroughly enjoyed by the audience. I laughed at times, and felt sadness at other times, because it was both funny and tragic.

Moscow had about one hundred and fifty different museums and permanent exhibitions. It would take the rest of this book to discuss all of them, but some of the most impressive was the Central Lenin Museum where the exhibit of Lenin's personal belongings were located, his desk, with secret drawers, a coat with bullet holes that were sustained after an attempted assassination, and his car. Another was the train of mourning at Paveletsky Railway Station, where the engine and carriage that brought the coffin with Lenin's body to Moscow. The Karl Marx and Frederick Engels Museum, which housed early documents and photographs of Marx and Engels with their close associates and friends, was imposing and included

Marx's personal belongings, such as his arm chair, and the easy chair in which he died in 1883.

We saw concerts and went shopping in Russia's largest department store, that was called at the time, GUM. All of this was inspiring and entertaining, but I was beginning to get a little restless, because we were constantly being directed and controlled by our guides. We went where they wanted us to go, and saw only what they wanted us to see. This was creating the desire within me to see the things that were not on our agenda.

After about a week in Moscow, we left for a town called Kalinin. It was about one hundred miles from Moscow on the upper Volga River. It was an ancient trading post. I was ready to leave Moscow, but I wasn't prepared for a four and a half hour bus trip that covered only a hundred miles. The bus traveled about thirty five miles an hour. Some of the roads were nearly impassable.

We had a new guide for this trip, and I sat beside her on the entire trip. She appeared to be about thirty five years old and charming, but guarded. For four and a half tiring hours, we talked about politics, philosophy, and our backgrounds. She was amused, and slightly disbelieving, when I told her of my life in the cotton mill village, my years with Kathrin, and my encounter in France. She wanted details and specifics of my life, but she was reserved and guarded about hers. I enjoyed talking with her, because I could playfully challenge some aspect of communism without her becoming annoyed. She became defensive, however, when I challenged the judicial system, which was made up of panels of judges, some of which had no legal training and the judical system had no juries. She recognized my rebellious nature and changed the subject by emphasizing rules and advising me of the seriousness of violations, especially about leaving the group for exploratory purposes on my own.

We got to our hotel in Kalinin about seven p.m., it was actually more like a motel. We were allowed about an hour to freshen up before dinner. The motel was named Motel Tver. Tver was originally the name of the town, but it was renamed Kalinin, which was the name of the President of the Soviet Union that served the first half of the twentieth century.

Upon our arrival, I had noticed a collective farm community across the highway from the motel, and I could see some of the people milling around on the old, frozen, dirt streets. I was determined to get into that village without the guide, so I began to plan.

That night, the Russians did everything they could to make us feel at home. They had a little group of musicians, who played American music, including *My Old Kentucky Home*, and a few more songs of that vintage. As with all Russian meals, vodka was plentiful, tap water would make you sick, so they had bottled water and vodka sitting on the table in full supply. After a long bus ride, we were ready to relax. I danced with my wife, and some of the other women in our group, including our Russian guide, but I couldn't get my mind off the collective farming community across the highway.

I had become friends with two other men in our group, and I felt that they shared my feeling of being too controlled. So that evening, the three of us plotted a plan to get up very early the next morning, before the group was scheduled to get together, and go across the street, without our guide, to tour the village and get some pictures. It never entered my mind that my actions might be detected by anyone else.

The idea was so exciting that we decided to drink some toasts to add to our adventure. I wanted orange juice to mix with the vodka. The bar custodian accommodated us with frozen orange juice that had to be mixed with water. He mixed it with tap water, which none of us noticed at the time. When I finally got to bed, the room was spinning so, that I had to put my foot on the floor to try to stabilize my stomach. It didn't work. I crawled on hands and knees to the toilet and vomited. I did finally fall asleep, but only for a few hours. When the alarm went off at four in the morning, I washed my face and put on my clothes quickly, to get to our rendezvous location at the side of the motel.

I was ready, although still a little dizzy, with my camera on my shoulder, but the excitement caused my blood to surge, and I felt good, in spite of the sickness. My friends didn't feel the same way. Only one showed up, and he was sickly pale, and was looking for a way to back-out gracefully. I ask him to just walk across the street to the village entrance with me and he could then go back. In return I promised to share my photos with him. He agreed, and apologized for not feeling well.

The village was beginning to come alive as dawn broke. The unpaved streets were frozen mud, and as hard as concrete. My friend wished me luck, turned around, and went back to the motel. I tried to look as Russian as I could, but it was obvious, to anyone in the village, that I was foreign. Having no televisions and few communications, other than the state controlled media, I reasoned that they would not know what an

American looked like, so with my Russian fur cap, I thought I could pull it off!

An old lady came up to the central well of the village to get water, she had a wooden yoke around her neck with a water pail on each end. I attempted to communicate with her, gesturing with my camera that I would like to get her picture. She smiled and nodded. Her face looked like weather-worn leather. When she smiled, all of the wrinkles deepened. Most of her teeth were missing, and those that were there, were brown. It was easy to see that this poor woman had worked the fields all of her life, and that life had been difficult.

When I was taking her picture, a man came up, obviously angry, he was scolding her very harshly. Pointing to the road and telling her to go back to her little cottage. She immediately turned back without getting her water.

He then began to scold me, I couldn't understand, but I could tell, by his tone and his facial expression, that it was time for me to move on.

Walking past a few more cottages, I suddenly heard the Russian National Anthem playing from speakers on poles and eves of some of the houses. I knew it was time to get back to the motel.

As I approached the field near the highway, I saw the KGB van. It was white with a huge black stripe across the middle and a horn blowing on and off like European police sounds. I knew I shouldn't run, so I leisurely walked across the field as though I was merely taking a morning stroll. They didn't buy it.

The agents, three of them, got out of the van and waited patiently for me. One of them spoke broken English, he asked for my camera, which I gratefully gave him hoping that would be the extent of the encounter. Unfortunately, it was only the beginning.

They carried me to the motel in the van, with the two agents sitting on each side of me while the other one drove. My mind went back to my experience in the Putnam County Jail in Tennessee, during my senior year at college. But this time I knew it was more serious. I began to think about those bland, Russian prisons, for spies that I had seen on television.

When we got to the motel, the entire motel staff was standing in the lobby, along with our guide. The tour group was waiting in the meeting room, away from the activity. Our guide came directly to me and shook her finger in my face and said, "I knew it was you! Do you realize how serious this is?" Now I was beginning to get really concerned.

They took me to a retaining area and contacted the U.S. Embassy in Moscow. The Embassy officials were not very happy with me, to say the least. The fun and excitement was gone, and I was beginning to get sick again. This time from the combination of fear and my hangover sickness. I was also humiliated, because when I went to the toilet to vomit, two agents went with me.

Our bus left for Leningrad without me. My wife thought I was going to a Russian prison. Fortunately, after diplomatic discussions between the U.S. Embassy in Moscow, and Russian KGB officials, the KGB escorted me to Leningrad to rejoin my group, but under close scrunity. They kept my camera and film, and gave me a firm reprimand. I was then under watchful eyes of the guides every minute of every day, all day, until we boarded the airplane to return to the United States.

Leningrad, formally St. Petersburg, was one of the most beautiful and elegant cities that I had ever visited. It was the second largest city in the U.S.S.R., and proudly claimed the name of "Venice of the North". Voltaire declared: "The united magnificence of all the cities of Europe, could not equal St. Petersburg." And the Russian poet Pushkin paid a tribute a century later: "I love you, Peter's great creation, your stately aspect, perfect ranks, the Neva River's undulation, the granite vestments of its banks." We toured the Hermitage museum of Russian Art, and many more cultural and historical areas. But the fun was gone, and it was time to return and get prepared to move into another life.

I was loaded with guilt on the flight from the Soviet Union. My first international trip associated with the Carter Administration, and I had botched it with my irresponsible, disregard of the protacol. I was in the process of preparing a letter of apology to the President and the Russian Foreign Minister when one of the State Department Officials came to my seat on the plane and told me to forget it. He said the President would never hear about it, and the issue would go no further. The Russians' primary concern, according to him, was that the pictures of Russian peasants would get published in U.S. newspapers and magazines, for propaganda purposes. However, I knew that there was more to their concern than that.

I could hardly get my mind off the old Russian woman in the collective farm village. She was probably only middle-aged, although she looked seventy-five. I had seen people, who aged like that, working in the cotton mills.

I felt a little sad as our plane lifted off the runway in Russia. It was early evening. I looked down at some of the collective villages, in the rural area of Western Russia, and wondered what they did at night.

I remembered the evenings in the mill village, after supper. The bats from the mill's inactive smoke stacks were out hunting for food, and we tossed rocks up into the air to watch their radar detecting the flying objects. They would dive at them, until they realized that the objects were rocks, and then they would peel off and climb out of the dive.

The village streets were dark, like the Russian villages, because the street lights were dim. They had small bulbs with a metal shade over them to protect them from the rain. They were extended to the center of the intersection, at every block, by the electric cords. The bulbs provided us nighttime target practice for our sling shots. I could imagine the kids, in the Russian collective farm villages, playing the same sort of games, and having the same sort of fun, without even realizing that their lives were difficult.

Element

6

Entrepreneur

Although I lost the Lt. Governors election, the loss pushed me further in the direction that I was already leaning. So I unconditionally submerged myself in the developing of Motels, Apartments, and Hotels. It was something that I knew nothing about, much the same as it was when I entered politics.

It was less than five years after I had finished college that I got my first development experience.

You would have thought we had won the lottery. We had just consummated our first business deal, without money or assets. We walked out of the office, of one of the wealthiest land owners in the county, in a very dignified business manner, keeping our composure until we got out of sight and sound. We then stopped the car and got out on the side of the road, jumped up and down, shouting, and slapping each other on the back, all the while bragging about what good businessmen we were.

An associate and I had just made our first business deal, and the only way we could accomplish it was to get the land owner to put up his land, and subordinate it to a mortgage of a health care facility. I still owed money for my college loan, and couldn't even afford to buy a house.

The idea for developing a health care facility was my friend's. We had met, and became associates, through the local Jaycee organization. We were both ambitious. He had read an article in a business magazine, about the founder of the Holiday Inn Corporation starting a new company, to develop health care facilities. Although we had no resources of our own, we decided to try to do it ourselves.

So we got a few local businessmen to put up some operating funds, quit our jobs, set up an office, and acted like successful entrepreneurs. Another one of our associates was a beginning architect, and he prepared the plans for construction, which made us appear much more organized than we actually were.

The last hitch now was to secure the land for the facility.

We set up a meeting with a wealthy landowner, hoping for a miracle, and we got one. It was my role to do the selling, so with authentic plans and architectural renderings, we began the process with a presentation. I knew that he had limited time, so I needed to keep things moving. I knew what I wanted to achieve, but I wasn't sure how to get there.

As I came to the end of the presentation, I stammered a little because I had to ask him to gamble his land on a risky business development. I did my best to be diplomatic as I told him that in order for us to purchase his land, we had to have control of it to get construction financing. I could see that he already understood. I falteringly said, "Do you know what I'm asking?" He responded that he understood what I wanted, and that he would take a chance because he had confidence in the development potential.

He instructed us to put the legal papers together for execution. We assured him that we would get them prepared, as we quietly folded up our documents, shook hands, and casually left the meeting in a very business-like manner, until we got out of his sight.

While we both had dabbled in small-time deals, this was the one that actually provided us with some degree of success. Before we started construction of the facility, a national health care organization bought it. Extendicare, Inc., a national corporation with stock traded on the New York Stock Exchange, traded us stock for the development. That transaction gave us a small amount of capital, and boosted our confidence.

After our success, I felt that I could do other deals, and that this one was only the beginning. The feeling was very similar to the feeling I had when my parachute opened on my first jump.

Although my business associate and I remained friends, serving in the Alabama Legislature, both the House and Senate, we never jointly developed any other projects.

For me, this was the first in a series of developments, some good, and some bad. I always tried to remember Kathrin's philosophy, "How can you lose, when you start with nothing." Actually, I started in the hole, as did everybody that came from the mill village. Her philosophy was that when your chances provide for either breaking even or winning, it was impossible to lose, and that life itself is the same.

I was beginning to have fun. This was the start of my sixth life.

My next development came while I was in the consulting business. An associate, in the national Model Cities Program, contacted me about developing an apartment complex in Huntsville. I agreed to assist, and got a substantial development fee and a contract to manage the apartments. It was easy, and I was hooked, but I was still torn between politics and business.

My second apartment development came while I was in the Alabama Senate in the mid 1970's. It was a large complex in Montgomery, Alabama. As usual, I hadn't concerned myself about the market potential, or whether the development would be successful. I just assumed that if I could get it financed, it would work. Consequently, my major concern was how to get it financed.

King Village groundbreaking

I was a leverage developer that is, I would leverage my interest in one development for financing on another.

When I discovered some financial syndicators in Birmingham, I knew that I could open the throttle and develop in high gear. These syndicators would raise capital by selling limited partnerships to high income individuals that needed tax shelters. So with the limited partners, all I had to do was tie down the land and get a financial commitment for a first mortgage, these mortgages were mostly non-recourse federally backed mortgages.

I was surprised that it was that easy, especially for someone with so little assets. I felt like I was playing monopoly again. So I plunged into the low cost land options and paper juggling with apartment syndicators for the next five years. During that period, I developed apartments, with a value of approximately twenty million dollars, with equity money from investors looking for tax shelters in developments that they would probably never see. The limited partners owned most of the equity, but then that's as it should be.

The development and management fees, with the residuals, gave me resources that I had never had before, so I focused on volume, because I enjoyed the challenge of having numerous negotiations and activities going at the same time. It reminded me of performers that kept numerous plates spinning on shafts simultaneously.

While I was enjoying the apartment development activities, I was still involved with politics, and still struggling with whether to go in one direction or the other.

The Lt. Governor's election was less than two years away, and I decided that I would run, since I had made a commitment to myself to continue in politics until my luck ran out.

I must admit that my heart wasn't in the campaign at the time. I was losing interest in politics, because I felt that it was a character deteriorating process. I sensed that the duplicity, and balancing acts required for campaigns, were corrosive, and my resoluteness had been tested enough in the five lifetimes I had already lived.

When I reflect on my previous existence's, I find that I conscientiously, or subconsciously, tended to put myself into predicaments that tested my survival, both physically and emotionally. These tests didn't always provide for monetary gain, although frequently it was an added benefit, but that was not my motivation. I usually focused more on the excitement of the development rather than the financial gain. I rarely hesitated to pledge everything that I owned on a new engaging project.

I think my mill village background, and my association with Kathrin, had laid the foundation for my acceptance of risk. Living in the mill village, and being a white boy living with a black female bootlegger in the deep south, exposed me to both sides of a culture where risk was common, even normal. So when I had an opportunity to switch my developing activities from apartments to hotels, I didn't hesitate.

I was in Pensacola, Florida, looking for apartment sites, when a local broker wanted to show me a motel site. I had a little time to spare, so I went with him to look at the property. It was located on the back side of a major shopping center, and it had exposure to a heavily traveled interstate. My first reaction was negative, because I didn't know anything about the lodging business, but the more I thought of it, the more positive the prospect became, and the more excited I got. I made arrangements to meet with a local motel operator, who liked the location, we structured a deal, and financed the development with a local bank. It was the first of a string of sixteen motels and hotels that I developed and operated.

Most of these developments occurred in the early eighty's. I managed to structure the deals by pledging equity in my existing properties so that I could get new developments financed. I was doing so many motel developments, during that time frame, that the management staff beseeched me to slow down so that they could catch up. By shifting funds and leveraging, we managed to come up with the initial capital to keep these properties operating, until they became self-sufficient. I was growing more confident each day.

As business expansion occured, especially with properties located in different cities, management by telephones and facsimiles, together with site visits and managers meetings, became the rule of operations.

With properties in four states, our annual managers meetings provided us with an opportunity to train and learn in group settings. The meetings were both business and social. They lasted about three days each.

The day sessions consisted mostly of training, and policy and procedure discussions. The evening sessions were more relaxed, with cocktails, dinner, and award presentations for best property, most improved, etc.

While the day sessions would sometimes get dry and boring, the evening sessions were set aside as fun events with some practical jokes and good natured kidding.

On one occasion, I became the unplanned joke of the evening. This event occurred at one of our largest manager's meetings in Oxford, Alabama.

We had completed the day training classes and were gathering in the Lounge for drinks, prior to going to dinner.

It was early evening around six. As we pulled about three tables together for drinks, I noticed a huge man sitting at the bar with a black (Nazi-style) motorcycle helmet on the stool beside him. He seemed to be interested in our group, because he focused his attention on our tables. He had a black bushy beard with eyebrows to match. His large, sleeveless arms were covered with tattoos, and he wore a black leather vest with motorcycle insignias covering most of the front.

I had remembered seeing a beautiful, black, Harley Davidson motorcycle parked outside the lounge, and I assumed it was his.

Everyone was aware of his focus on our table, but I think we all assumed that he was just curious, that is until he began to smile and nod. At that point I had the feeling that he was flirting with one of the female managers.

There were a few other "happy-hour" customers in the lounge and the jukebox music was playing, but nobody was dancing at this early hour.

Suddenly he pulled himself off the bar stool and lumbered across the floor to the jukebox. After making a few selections, he turned and started toward our table, still smiling and rocking a little with the music, as if he wanted to dance.

One of the females, sitting next to me, was beginning to get uneasy because it appeared as if he was directing his smiles and body language for her benefit. He seemed so friendly that it was difficult not to return his smile, which was probably a mistake. Encouraged, he began to make his way across the floor to our table. As he approached the table, I nudged her arm and whispered, "Prepare yourself".

He swaggered around the table, to the side where she was sitting, and reached his hand out toward me. I assumed that he was going to introduce himself to me and get permission to ask her to dance. Instead he took MY hand and asked ME to dance. At first I was completely speechless, and then I thought someone had set me up for a joke, so I politely thanked him but said no.

I could feel everyone's eyes on me, and I was embarrassed. Still holding on to my hand, he looked into my eyes and whispered, "I love you". I could feel my face burning as I stammered uncertainly, that I loved him too, but I didn't want to dance. He then planted a big wet kiss on the back of my hand before he let it go.

Most of the onlookers tried to be casual or nonchalant, but I knew they were struggling to keep from laughing.

Our group left the lounge shortly afterwards, and the motorcyclist threw me another big kiss, as I anxiously hurried out the door.

Perhaps it was this sense of humor, and my love for the edge, that led me into an entirely new business venture.

It happened in the early eighties, when people were going to lounges in record numbers. Especially those night spots that promoted music, dancing, and free buffets.

I was in the process of buying a motel in Montgomery, Alabama. Strangely, this was the motel where I stayed when I was in the Senate, during the time that I slipped and dislocated my shoulder on my first day of the session.

The motel was losing money, but I felt that it had potential, especially if I could convert the "home style" restaurant into a popular lounge concept.

The lounges that were financially successful, during the early eighties, were the ones with a theme. One such successful theme was the 1960s diner style, which played the music of the sixties, and the waiters and waitresses did dance routines to encourage customers to dance.

I kept the motel purchase negotiations in limbo while I traveled the major cities in the south to get ideas about the concept. I was particularly impressed with certain lounges with the sixties style decor. They were colorful and successful, so I decided to proceed with that idea.

I needed a catchy name that would fit. One day, while driving back from Montgomery, I was listening to an oldies radio station, and I heard the name of my soon-to-be lounge. It was "Staggerlees". When I heard the song, I was certain that it would identify with the sixties sound.

I knew that the concept was high risk, because Montgomery was primarily a country music town. But I reasoned that if the lounge was successful, the motel rooms would fill.

With the lounge idea in mind, I began to negotiate seriously and consummated the acquisition of the motel within thirty days.

It turned out to be the first of five successful *Staggerlees Lounges.* This one was by far the most profitable, with people sometimes forming long lines outside waiting to get in, especially on Wednesdays, Fridays and Saturdays.

The motel's occupancy immediately went up, because the traveling business clientele loved the lounge and didn't want to drive after having a few drinks.

Success seemed to be coming from every direction with new deals in progress. My confidence was soaring and I thought I couldn't miss. It was this attitude that brought on the biggest failure of my development career.

It must have been about four in the morning, I was stunned and sat up immediately in my bed. Kathrin was standing at the foot of my bed. She had been deceased for about five years, yet her appearance was exactly the way she looked when I had lived with her during my childhood.

I had finally slept for the first time in about three weeks, and I was exhausted, both mentally and physically, and I thought my mind was playing tricks. Her eyes looked directly at me, and without any sign of emotion she said, "JUST GET ON WITH IT"! I knew instantly what she was talking about. She used the same tone, and expression, when she said that to me on my return from France.

My self-assured attitude had been deflated. I had been struggling for almost a year over a failed development that was taking its toll. My "carefree"development philosophy had diminished. I didn't think I could recover financially. Instead of the attitude I had years earlier, when I simply felt that I would "do another deal" and move on, this time I was stuck.

I had accumulated some financial resources, and I was ready to go to New Zealand for my next life when I got the impulse to purchase a big hotel in downtown Birmingham. It was the biggest deal that I had ever done, and I was sure, as always, that it would be successful.

The hotel had once been the most prestigious hotel in Alabama. It had hosted many famous people and celebrities, including President Richard Nixon, Alabama Football Coach Bear Bryant, movie star Doris Day and O.J. Simpson. It had been closed for about two years, following a foreclosure by a Tennessee bank.

My business logic was seduced by nostalgia. I could visualize this old hotel coming back to its sixties heyday; this was 1994.

After many unsuccessful attempts, we finally got the development financed. The bank required that I put up everything that I owned as collateral. Never allowing myself to doubt for a second that the hotel would be a success, I agreed to do it.

Everything that could have gone wrong did. The general contractor couldn't get the construction finished on time, delaying the opening for a year. Another contractor had to be engaged, which caused a million dollar cost overrun. The opening was a catastrophe, and the losses kept piling up at astronomical rates.

I had to sell most of my other properties to stay solvent, and I seriously looked at bankruptcy for almost a year.

Somehow, I had lost that optimism that I always had before. Maybe, it was because I was older, and getting more conservative, or maybe I was ready to move into another life. Whatever the reason, I couldn't shake the depression.

Fortunately, the bank thought the hotel was worth the mortgage balanced owed, so they took the property and released me from personal guarantees. So again, I dodged the bullet, but not without significant losses.

Kathrin had communicated with me that morning, as she had so often before, with unbounded wisdom. She had made me understand how fortunate I was to have experienced the limits of life, and that I hadn't really lost anything because I started with nothing.

I got out of bed and sat on my deck until daylight, thinking of how much I cared for her and hearing her words, over and over again, as I had heard so many times before, when she sensed that I was losing it.

"Just get on with it", rang in my ears.

As the sun peeped over the mountain, dispersing the shadows, I felt refreshed and rested, after almost a year of struggle and months of exhaustion. I had lost nearly three million dollars on the hotel, but had I truly lost anything? Not really, I didn't have a dime when I started. I had experienced a tremendous roller coaster ride.

Had I been born to a family with financial resources, or inherited wealth, I wonder if I would have pushed the envelope to the extent of leveraging all of it on one development? I doubt it.

I knew that I had to roll the dice and take the risks. I didn't have to carry the burden that I might have squandered money that my ancestors had accumulated, through their own initiative and hard work. At least, resources that I put at risk were those that were accumulated by my own efforts, and with few exceptions, I had a good time. I was negotiating another deal within a month, and consummated it within the year.

Anyway, I had already had more than twenty years of development exposure, some bad, but mostly good, and I had gained in spite of it all.

I was ready for my next life.

Element

7

Confronting Fear

My entire life flashed before me when I backed over the side of a construction crane platform, one hundred and thirty feet from the ground, the equivalent of a thirteen story building. It must have been a horrifying sight, because I could hear people screaming and yelling. I was falling, head first, at a rate of one hundred and twenty miles an hour. I was vaguely aware of the people standing on the ground, and they appeared to be upside down, as my conscientiousness tried to leave me.

Its strange that, in such a few short seconds, so many things can zip through the mind. I wondered what the impact would feel like, or if I would even be aware. Would there be any pain, would it hurt, or be instant nothingness, as I had often heard.

Suddenly, it felt as if the speed of my decent was beginning to slow. It was as though some magical power had intervened before I hit the ground, letting me experience this in slow motion. My rate of fall was clearly slowing, and I became upright. I could then see the shocked faces of people standing on the ground.

My fall came to a complete stop at, what appeared to be, ten feet before impact. Slowly, I started to ascend, gradually at first, then at a high rate of speed, as though I had been gently caught and tossed, by some unseen force, back toward the construction platform. The yell I was now hearing was mine, as I flew upward past loose sections of a dangling bungee cord. I knew in that instant that I would live to do it again.

Why was I compelled, time and again, to walk that thin line between life and death. I knew it couldn't be a mid-life crisis, because it began when I was a child, and it didn't end with my childhood.

This need, to confront my fear, has been my companion, and nemesis, throughout my various lifetimes.

Part II

Walking in Nashville

Spring 1985, on a Greyhound Bus, Thursday three p.m., enroute from Huntsville to Nashville for a four day life as a "street person" on the sidewalks and in the alley's.

I was living alone in an apartment complex that I had developed in Huntsville. I had planned the trip for months, only to have to reschedule, two or three times, because of pressing business. I was in the process of selling my apartments at the time, and the negotiations were getting bogged down. My company was operating five apartment complexes and eleven hotels, and I was ready to put the apartment business behind me. Eight years was about the extent of my interest in any one endeavor. I felt that I had been reasonably successful developing apartments, in spite of my limited resources. I now wanted to devote my time to hotel development.

The Nashville excursion was one that I had not shared with any other person. I had never mentioned, even to Kathrin, nor my family, of my desire to experience living on the street in a large city. This secret was about to explode within me, but I was determined that it would be concealed until I returned.

I considered Birmingham, Atlanta, and Nashville, as possible destinations. Nashville was my choice, because I had business and political associates in Birmingham and Atlanta, and I didn't want to take a chance on seeing anyone that I knew. If the experience was going to be worthwhile, I had to structure it so that I couldn't adjust the circumstances, even when, and if, things became difficult. In order to do that, I had to leave all identification behind, including my drivers license. I also had to leave credit cards, checks, and any other sources of financial support. I wanted to eliminate the possibility of getting immediate funds, which could be used to ease the difficulties of the experience.

I parked my car, three blocks away, on an apartment parking lot, and walked to the bus station. I purchased a round trip ticket to Nashville, which took a large part of my total cash resources of thirty dollars. I carried only a small hand bag containing a toothbrush, toothpaste, and a couple of cigars.

I was excited, and eager, to get started, though a little apprehensive. After twenty minutes, on the road, the rain started, not a sprinkle, but a downpour. I knew it was too late to turn back, besides I had already made a commitment to myself that, irrespective of what happened, I was going to live these four days on the street without alternatives, and I was determined that nothing would alter my plan.

When I got off the bus, at the Greyhound Station, in Nashville, I realized that there was nothing to do but hangout for the next four days. There was a sense of excitement at being somewhere without anyone's knowledge. I had told the Vice President of my company that I would be gone for a few days, and that I wouldn't be contacting the office, nor did I wish to be contacted. He seemed a little puzzled, but he didn't press me. In addition to being the Vice President, he was also a personal friend, and he knew when I didn't want to be challenged.

I stopped at the snack bar, in the bus station, and got a cup of coffee and a donut. I was stunned when I realized that I only had fifteen dollars and some change left, and I still had three and half days to go.

I then understood something I had long forgotten, that simple things that I took for granted, a cup of coffee, and a donut, was a big expense item to people who are poor. This was just the beginning.

I sat in the bus station waiting room for a couple of hours, because it was raining, and the people were interesting to watch. I noticed that the security officer occasionally would check for tickets in the waiting room, because "street people" would often come in and sleep on the benches in the waiting area, especially when it was raining. Even though I had my return ticket, I didn't want to wear out my welcome.

It was about eleven p.m. when I left the station. I didn't know where to go, so I drifted down the street for a few blocks. I noticed some warehouses along the railroad tracks, and I decided to make my first night there. It seemed safe, and I could get on the dock of a warehouse out of the steady drizzle of rain.

The warehouse dock was about five feet from the ground, and about thirty feet from the railroad track. There were no lights, and I didn't see a night watchman. So I hopped up on the dock and begin to prepare for the first night at my new home. The dock was dry, and the rain was beginning to pick up a bit.

I found a couple of empty wooden platforms there, the type used to stack boxes, etc., for forklifts to move around. I moved them close together, and against the warehouse wall. My mattress was a couple of pieces of cardboard boxes, that I found on the dock. I put them over the wooden slats, on the platforms, and stretched my tired body out on my new bed. I lighted a small cigar, that I had packed away in my little bag, and snacked on the other half of the donut that I had saved from the bus station snack bar.

I could hear the rain beating down on the metal walls and roof of the warehouse, and it actually seemed cozy.

Just as I was drifting off to sleep, I heard the sound of men's voices. It first sounded as if they were directly across the tracks, but then their voices seemed to fade slightly in the distance, as though they were moving away. I started to feel uneasy when I saw the glare of automobile lights.

I got off my makeshift bed and went to the edge of the dock, concealing myself behind the warehouse wall, I cautiously peeped out to see if I could tell what was happening. A police car pulled down near the tracks on the opposite side with the head lights still shining.

Two policemen got out of the car and walked around the area. One of them had a flashlight, and he was directing its beam into the bushes. After a few minutes they got back into the car, backed up the hill, and drove off. I was uneasy, but I didn't dare move.

Within ten minutes, the police car pulled up beside the warehouse where I was located. They again stopped and got out of the car, but they never came over to the warehouse dock. After ten minutes or so, they left and didn't come back during the remainder of the night, but I couldn't sleep.

My clothes were still wet from the rain when I got up to leave at four in the morning. My back and legs were aching.

I knew that I could be arrested for trespassing, and since I didn't have any identification, I could be arrested for vagrancy too.

I went back to the bus station for a cup of coffee, and was relieved to see that the security guard had changed shifts. So I enjoyed a couple of hours in the dry bus terminal. It gave me a chance to wash my face and brush my teeth. My hair was matted down, my clothes damp and wrinkled, and I looked very much like a street person, and still had two and a half days to go.

The rain stopped, and the clouds cleared about ten a.m. The warm sun helped to dry my clothes.

I walked through many streets in downtown Nashville, and eventually found my way to the State Capitol. The legislature was in session, but it had recessed for the weekend. The legislative chambers were open, and a few of the members were still wrapping things up for the week.

I asked one of the security guards if I could look into the Senate chambers, and he nodded while curiously looking me over. I was impressed with the elegance of the Senate chambers. I reflected a little on my own experiences in the Alabama Senate while standing there.

As I was leaving the Tennessee Senate chamber, I couldn't resist telling the security guard that I had served in the Alabama Senate for four years. He just nodded his head.

The sun had dried the grass around the State Capitol, so I laid down on the soft dry grass and read a copy of the Nashville Banner, that I found on a bench, and relaxed for a few hours, dozing off a couple of times.

My food came from convenience stores for the next three days; water, peanut butter crackers, and potato chips. I was hungry the entire trip.

It was easy to go unnoticed in downtown Nashville during the day, but late night was more difficult.

I decided to find a place to sleep for the night while the sun was still shining. I knew I could always go back to the warehouse, but I didn't think my back could handle it. I found an office building that was under construction, about two miles from the bus terminal, with easy access under the front steps. Actually, there was a small sheltered area underneath the steps, and it was far enough away from the sidewalk to prevent my being seen by pedestrians.

When I found some Styrofoam pieces and cardboard, I knew I was going to have a decent pad for the night. The construction crew had already quit for the day, it was around four in the afternoon, so I had a few hours to drift.

I was actually beginning to enjoy the experience, except that I wanted to eat something substantial, but I only had thirteen dollars and seventy-five cents left, so I knew that I had to put my mind on something else.

It was difficult enough not having a wallet, a watch, or any kind of identification, but being unable to take a shower was a major problem. My hair was beginning to look and feel greasy and stiff.

I thought that if I could get to "Printers Alley", I could get lost in the activity, because it was the center of night club-lounge activity in Nashville, and people would be moving to and from the clubs, paying little attention to others.

I was wrong. I could feel the apprehension from people walking in the area. I had worn a light colored, almost white, water repellent windbreaker, and it had become so filthy, from my night on the warehouse dock, that I looked dangerous. I noticed some of the doormen focusing on me when I lingered, so I decided to keep moving.

I began to feel like a fugitive, as I walked the downtown streets of Nashville at night. I was practically alone on the streets after eleven p.m., and I knew that if the police began to notice me, they might ask for identification. I also knew that I could be arrested, so I began to duck into alleys when I saw a police car coming down the street. I also got very uneasy if a policeman came into a convenience store when I was there. Although I was completely innocent, I began to act like a guilty person.

I decided that the best place I could be was out of sight. I was ready to crawl under the steps at the construction site and go to sleep. I made a decent pad, with the Styrofoam and cardboard, and slept soundly until daybreak, which was about five a.m.

Saturday was much like Friday, I just drifted around downtown and the bus terminal area, occasionally being scrutinized by other "street people". I was beginning to comprehend something, and that was literally how vulnerable I had become. On the one hand, I was afraid the police would arrest me, and on the other, I realized that sleeping on the streets could make me an easy target for unscrupulous people, so I began to get a little paranoid.

As Sunday came, I was really getting self-conscious. I smelled terrible, looked worse, and it was becoming increasingly difficult to gain access to service stations and convenience stores, for the purpose of using the toilet and brushing my teeth. I could imagine how the attendants felt when they saw me walking up with my mangy hair, filthy clothes, unpleasant smell, and carrying a small bag. I also noticed the anxious eyes of store clerks when I bought crackers or chips.

When the rain started again, on Sunday night, I was happy. I wanted to get wet and I walked the streets in the rain.

I had my biggest test that Sunday night as I walked past a downtown hotel. I was soaked, tired, hungry, and dirty. I could see the fresh, clean people, either sitting in the lounge chairs or going into the restaurant for a drink and dinner. I knew that I could make a few phone calls, if I could get to a phone, and stay the rest of the night in the comfort of this luxury hotel with a fine dinner. But I wasn't about to throw-in the towel with only one day to go.

I went back to the bus terminal area and sat under a local bus stop shed to dry out. The rain had stopped.

I had previously noticed two men, obviously street people, around the bus terminal, because they began to acknowledge me, when we passed each other, during the last couple of days. They were a curious looking couple, one tall and skinny, and the other short and fat. They both carried worn paper bags with the top rolled down.

They stopped at the bus stop shed to talk with me. They asked me where I was headed. I said to the bus station. They smelled of cheap wine and body odor, but they seemed friendly. I don't think they believed I was catching a bus, because they invited me to go with them to the bottom of the hill where they had set up for the night. I declined by saying my bus would be leaving within the next hour.

They bid me good night, and started walking down the deserted street singing loudly, *Your Cheatin Heart*. As I watched them disappear into the hazy night, I could still see their arms locked, and faintly hear them singing. I wished at that moment, that I had a camera, because I knew it would be difficult to relate that unusual and joyful experience. I had made the grade, I had been accepted by bone-a-fide street people as one of them.

Finally, the bus pulled into the Huntsville Greyhound Station at ten a.m. on Monday, four days after I had left home to become a street person. Understandably, I had a seat to myself, and I slept all the way. I walked the few blocks to my car, in the apartment parking space, with my head down, hoping that nobody would recognize me.

I drove straight to my apartment, grabbed my door keys from under the dash, and actually ran to my unit, before disappearing inside. I had about ten messages on my answering machine, two of them were panic messages from the Vice President of my company. I immediately called him and ask him to come to my apartment and I would go into details about the previous four days.

I had enough time to get a long shower before he arrived, and I was stuffing food into my mouth as fast as I could.

He sat staring at me for an hour without uttering a word, as I told him the story of my adventure. When I finished, he studied me for another minute or so and said "You're crazy!"

Nashville gave me enough time on the street, now I needed the air.

Part III

Parachute

Ever since I flew over my grandmother's boarding house, in a corrugated box, I knew I could fly.

It was a three year old child's dream, but it was lucid. Even after more than five decades, I can still feel the sensation, when the box began to slowly spin around, as it lifted off the ground. I remember looking down into the coal-soot coated chimney, as I passed over the top of the roof. The decent was breath taking, the spinning had stopped, and I softly settled down in my Grandfather's small vegetable garden. The gentle bump, as the box touched the ground, woke me, but the experience never left me.

Even as I dangled in a parachute harness, in a hanger at a small airfield in Millbrook, Alabama, I would revisit the experience of my dream, and feel my pulse accelerate.

After four weekends of training, our weekend for the first jump had arrived. We had jumped from ten foot heights to learn to distribute our weight, as we hit the ground, from our feet, along the calf, thigh, butt, and shoulder, in a rolling fashion. My crotch was still sore and bruised from hanging in the parachute harness while learning what to do in case of malfunctions. I was so excited that I didn't sleep at all the night before the jump.

I went through the training with two others. We each had been assigned a number, and performed in that sequence. I was second in the order of training and jumping.

On a hot, July morning we waited beside the small, unstable look-ing aircraft. I noticed that the pilot's eyes could hardly focus. I wondered if he had a physical problem, or was taking some uncontrolled substance.

Our jump master lectured us, for a brief ten minutes, giving us our last minute instructions, and then said emphatically, that if we got in the plane we were going to jump, as if I needed anything else to raise my heart rate after looking at the pilot. He also gave us a face-saving way out. He said, "I can understand if you had a bad night, or if you do not feel ready, and want to postpone your first jump for another time, BUT, if you get on the plane today, be prepared to jump!"

The plane had only one seat, and it belonged to the pilot. The three of us, along with the jump master, sat on the floor. The temperature was about a hundred degrees, and the humidity was heavy. Everyone was wet with perspiration. The space was so small that we had to face each other with our knees pulled up, jamming our reserve chutes against our chests while hyperventilating.

The jump master opened the airplane side door at an altitude of about eleven hundred feet to allow us to adjust to the engine roar and the wind noise. As I looked around the shoulders of my friend, down at the tiny cars and little houses on the landscape below, I could barely get enough air into my lungs.

The jump master gave us our last minute instructions as we reached three thousand feet. He went through each of the commands beginning with the "jump position". On this command, the first jumper was sup-posed to move to the open door of the airplane and place his feet out of the door onto a small strut that extended two feet out from the bottom of the airplane. His instructions continued, "out under the wing" meant that the jumper had to reach his left arm out and up to grip the wing brace. The wings of the plane were situated on the top of the cockpit, so that the jumper had to pull himself out of the plane with his left hand, and then reach upward with his right hand to take hold of the wing brace, while simultaneously turning his feet on the base strut so that he was facing the forward direction of the plane. This maneuver alone was energy draining, and when combined with the wind velocity and engine noise, it became a very difficult task. It was almost a relief to hear the Jump Master shout, "jump".

Upon the command, "jump position", the first jumper was supposed to move into position, but he didn't move when the jump master commanded. He then leaned into his face and shouted the command again with no results, finally on the third command, the first jumper slid over to the door on his butt, and proceeded through the sequence.

The actual jump wasn't as frightening as having to crawl out under the wing, while trying to avoid looking down at the ground three thousand feet below.

On our first jump, we were on a static jump line, which automatically opened the parachute after we cleared the tail of the plane.

I don't remember if I was conscious for the first five seconds after I left the plane, but suddenly, the parachute opened and the engine noise was gone. I was floating like a feather in the beautiful July sunshine. I knew then, that the worse thing that could happen to me, was a broken ankle or leg, but I would live to experience it again.

The natural high from the jump was a tremendous feeling that stayed with me for two days. My landing was perfect, and I jumped up and down and yelled, although I was all alone in the soybean field.

The three of us would soon fly ultralight airplanes together. We became risk-taking friends, although they never, to my knowledge, tried another parachute jump. I continued.

On my third jump, my first without a static line, everything seemed easy, and my confidence had grown with each jump.

This time however, I decided to steer my landing near the truck, which was usually parked about a half mile away from where I landed. In the heat of the July sun in Alabama, carrying that chute a half mile was a struggle. So as soon as my chute opened, I began to try to spot the jump truck so that I could guide myself within a few hundred feet of it. I had planned to show off my skill and save a long hot walk to boot.

When I spotted the truck near the asphalt runway, I thought it would be easy, and it was. That is until I got within a thousand feet of the ground.

I was jumping at a rural, uncontrolled airport where airplanes fly in and out at will, without any clearance instructions from a flight control station. We had been unofficially warned that the plane pilots were unhappy with the sky diving activities in the area, and that if we continued to jump there, we were at risk of encountering aircraft in flight.

As I confidently drifted toward the dive truck, I heard the sound of an airplane engine revving up to a high pitch, as it does on take-off. I looked down between my legs and I saw a small single engine plane lifting off the runway just below me. The noise was deafening, and the turbulence caused me to loose control of my steering. I pulled my lines hard to try to slow my decent. I was swinging like a pendulum beneath the chute, and only about a hundred feet above the runway.

Our trainers had cautioned us about four things that we should avoid in parachuting. They were; water, power lines, trees, and yes, paved areas.

The last thing I remember, before hitting the runway, was that I was on the upswing of the pendulum, just before I started the downswing, and then I HIT. I had, in fact hit with the combination of speed from the downswing, and the parachute decent.

When I finally regained consciousness, the driver of the jump truck was loosening my gear and holding my chute, which had been dragging my body down the runway. My helmet was smashed, my pants and boots were torn off, and the left side of my body, from my shoulder to my ankle, was cut and bruised. Fortunately, nothing was broken.

The jump master wanted me to go to the emergency room at the hospital, but I wanted to go home. They helped me into my car, and I drove two hundred miles to Huntsville.

The drive to Huntsville was painful, but at times, actually amusing. I had hoped to make it home without stopping, but I had to urinate and the pressure was overwhelming. By the time I got to the Cullman, Alabama Interstate Exit, which was about sixty miles from Huntsville, I had to stop.

I knew that I looked grotesque so I drove around the convenience store to the back of the building. The restroom, which was located in the back, had an outside entrance. So I pulled my car up to the door to avoid being seen by anyone.

It must have taken me ten minutes to get out of the car, because I was stiff and my left leg would not bend. I struggled toward the restroom door, dragging my left leg. My jumpsuit was torn open, from my hip to my ankle, and my bare leg and foot had dried blood and bruises that were exposed. The left side of my face was swollen, and there were abrasions on my cheek.

When I reached for the restroom door handle, an elderly man was simultaneously opening the door to come out. He looked at me, gasped, and pulled the door closed. It took another three minutes to explain to him, through the door, that I had a parachute accident, and that I was harmless. He finally slid out and around the door, still looking over his shoulder at me, as he swiftly scurried away.

Several huge trucks passed my car on the highway. Some of the drivers would look down, taking a quick glance, no doubt anticipating seeing some exposed female leg and cleavage. Instead, they saw a battered male in severe pain. Their shocked expressions almost made me laugh in spite of the pain.

I was so stiff and sore, when I finally got home, that I couldn't get out of the car without assistance. After soaking in my bathtub for a couple hours, I crawled into bed, and stayed there for two days.

It seemed that my childhood dream of flying continued to push me to experience the reality. Within a few months, following the incident, I was again flying. This time on a snow covered mountain in Huntsville.

Part IV

Snow Sledding

My eyes were beginning to focus, but I still couldn't make out the faces of the people standing over me. Gradually I began to recognize my son, and my daughter's boyfriend, then slowly the other guys became familiar. My body had just sailed about twenty-five feet into the air, collided with a traffic sign, and spun into a five foot ditch filled with snow. I had been unconscious for about five minutes. It happened in January, 1986 about three a.m. on the side of Monte Sano Mountain in Huntsville. We had been snow sledding down the side of the mountain since about ten p.m.

It was one of those rare Alabama winters when we got a heavy snow that didn't melt as soon as it hit the ground. This one came late in the day, and the mountain was very cold. In fact, the temperature was about fifteen degrees and the snow on the sledding trail was like hard ice, and you could hear it cracking under the weight of the sled.

The sledding trail actually was a street covered with snow and packed by a few vehicles that ventured on it after the snow started, packing it down into an ice sheet. The trail was about five miles of slopes and sharp curves, and at top speed, the sleds were going so fast that tears would stream out of our eyes and freeze in our ears.

We didn't have enough sleds, so on many rides, we would double up, one person lying on the bottom and the other, on top. On some of the double curves, it was almost impossible to recover coming out of one before banking into another. It wasn't easy to get to the bottom of the trail without flipping over at least once.

It had always been a ritual, when the snow came in North Alabama and Huntsville, a certain regular group would drive jeeps and four wheel drive vehicles with snow sleds to the top of the mountain and sled all night. I was there with a group of friends.

It was impossible to get back to the top of the mountain without a vehicle. We used an old Ford truck hood turned upside down with a steel cable connected to the front and attached to the rear end of a Jeep. The cable was about thirty-five feet long.

I didn't realize what a ride I was in for when I piled on the makeshift sled, with about six other guys, heading back up the mountain at about three a.m. The combination of numbness from the cold and Jack Daniels whisky had made it impossible to feel anything, especially with the excitement of being able to sled down the mountain again, after we reached the top. After about five hours, of exhaustive sledding combined with whiskey, we were getting careless.

I got on the old hood sled last, so I had to reach over the guys in front to get a hold. Our driver seemed to get a little faster and more reckless each time. This time he was really pressing it. The ride up the mountain was almost as much fun as the ride down. As the jeep picked up speed, the shouting and laughter picked up too. The driver was looking back most of the time. Suddenly, he was into the double curve without realizing it. He was struggling to keep control of the jeep. As we came out of the first curve, the sled was in a whipping motion, and it became airborne, flying about eight feet into the air.

I remembered hitting the curve warning sign, but nothing else, until I became aware of faces drifting into my vision. There were hands shaking me, and voices asking if I was all right.

My body was so numb from the cold that I was not aware of any injuries. I knew I would be sore, and probably bruised, but I expected that anyway. So after regaining sufficient coordination, I climbed back on the hood, with the other guys slapping me on the back to encourage me, as we went back to the top again.

I enjoyed the thrill of sledding down the mountain at least two more times.

As dawn was beginning to break, we departed the magnificent mountain to go home and get some rest.

My daughter and her girlfriend had stayed in my apartment, and were asleep on the couches when we got there.

After they left, I filled my bathtub with hot water so that I could thaw out and soak, hoping to avoid some of the soreness I knew that I would have from the collision. It was not until I started peeling off the layers of my clothing that I realized I was bleeding. I had a hole in my thigh, just below my hip, the size of a fifty cent piece, where the metal bolt on the back of the road sign had punctured it. I had noticed the hole torn in my jeans, but I didn't realize the damage the impact had done to my leg. Blood was on my upper leg, and had run all the way down into my socks. The wound had the appearance of what I imagined a gun shot would look like.

I cleaned my injury, and soaked for an hour in the hot steaming bath, before getting out and collapsing on my bed. Five hours later I awoke, but I was so stiff and sore that I could hardly move.

I didn't go to a Doctor, because I had heard that a puncture wound was better left open so that it can heal from within. It must have been true, because in about two weeks I was as good as ever.

A puncture scar is very obvious, and this one can be seen when I wear swim shorts. I often get asked what caused it. At first, in jest, I would say that it was a shark bite, just for the reaction, but then when I would tell them the actual facts they seemed more amused than with the shark story. So I dropped the shark story.

I had enough ice and snow for awhile and I wanted hot sun and water.

Part V

Scuba

Just eighteen months later, the freezing cold hill became the deck of a scuba diving boat on an unbearably hot day.

It must have been one hundred and fifteen degrees, on the dive boat, just off the Grand Cayman Islands. My head was spinning, the boat was spinning, and I was nauseated. I had been a certified scuba diver for five years, and I had just done something very stupid and totally against the training I had received.

My dive group was doing a deep dive, about a hundred feet. During the dive, I got separated from the rest of the group including my dive buddy, who happened to be my son. Occasionally I would get distracted, by the exotic fish or coral reefs, and drift away from my group, as was the case this time. But this was the first time that I actually got lost.

It was June, 1987, and I was wondering, while lying on the deck of the ship, if I would ever dive again. I had ascended too quickly, without stopping long enough to decompress, and I had a minor case of the "bends". One rule that I did follow however, is the one that requires the diver to surface, should he get lost from his dive buddy or group, and cannot locate them within sixty seconds. In my haste and carelessness, I had just surfaced too quickly.

The bends is a simple case of nitrogen getting compressed into the blood stream. In some cases, people have to be flown to a hospital equipped with decompression facilities. I was lucky, once again, because

175

my case wasn't that bad. This was my third diving injury, not counting all the little bruises and cuts, and I was getting discouraged.

My first was a punctured ear drum, which had to be surgically repaired. The second was a torn stomach muscle, that happened when I was boarding the dive boat in the Bahamas. I was caught in a strained position, as my air tank got twisted on my back, when I was coming out of the water. The strain caused my back to arch, and my stomach muscle to tear and separate. The injury also required surgery to knit the muscle back together.

Now, I was struggling with a mild case of the bends and wondering whether I should just give up. But as the beautiful panorama of colors and underwater sights drifted through my memory, I knew that I would not quit.

In fact, just the day before this incident, I was feeding sting rays that were sitting on the bottom of a lagoon about thirty-five feet down. Our group was given squid, and told to sit on the bottom, because the sting rays may come at you from any angle, and you had to protect certain areas of the body. For males, sitting on the bottom was especially important.

The sting rays seemed playful as they dove in from behind, above, and from the side. Since their eyes were on the top of their head, and their mouths on the bottom, the squid, had to be shoved into their mouths from below. Their mouths functioned like a water vacuum, sucking the food up.

In a few seconds they were coming from every angle. We began to test them after a while, pushing them away. They seemed to be returning the playfulness, and in one particular incident, they knocked me completely upside down.

I had never experienced this kind of closeness to a sea animal, and this was one of the reasons that I knew I would continue diving.

Lying on my back, on the dive boat, I began to think about all of my wonderful diving adventures. Such as the one that happened about a year ago, while diving off Roatan Island in Honduras, when our divers encroached on a moray el's territory. It was clearly unhappy, when it came out from under a rock ledge, with its mouth opening and closing to show its teeth, trying to intimidate us enough that we would clear out. We did, but we again had experienced a special kind of closeness with a creature from another world.

Night dives were by far the most beautiful. The colors of the sea are much more discernible at night, making the entire dive a fantasy. I closed my eyes and experienced the suction cups of a small octopus, that I picked up off a coral ledge on a night dive. It wrapped its tentacles around my arm and the small cups felt like tiny vacuums as I pulled it off and eased it back onto the coral so that it could continue its journey for food.

My most startling diving experience, however, came during a night dive in Honduras. I was diving by a steep rock cliff. I was facing the cliff, and very slowly descending, when I came to a large overhanging ledge. When I drifted below the ledge, I was so startled that I almost blew the regulator out of my mouth. I had come face to face with the biggest grouper I could imagine. It was probably magnified by my mask and the water, but it looked to be six feet long and three feet thick. Groupers are not harmful, but the sheer size of the fish was jolting. I quickly moved up a few feet where my son was diving, to get his attention. I motioned for him to come down to see the grouper, he was as stunned as I. The grouper looked as though it was asleep, except that its huge eyes stared directly at us. It was deadly still, not even a fin moved.

While most sea life is domicile at night, there are exceptions, we experienced that in the Bahamas when I was on a group night dive. As we began our decent, one of the divers surprised a large baracuda, about thirty feet below the surface. He focused his flashlight on it to allow the other divers to see. Then all of them held their flashlights on it, obviously afraid to let it get out of sight.

We had unconsciencously encircled the fish, and it felt trapped within the circle of lights. It was frightened and becoming agitated. Its mouth was opening and closing in defiance to the lights. When I realized that it needed a dark area within the enclosure to allow it to escape, I turned my flashlight off. That caused it to thrust directly toward me. I bit down hard on my air regulator, and jerked my feet upward, hoping that I wouldn't feel those sharp teeth. I felt the turbulence of the water just under my legs as it broke away. It must have been about three feet long, but it was those sharp teeth that had me concerned.

As the dive boat rocked back and forth, and my head spun, I thought about one of my most unusual diving experiences at Crystal River, Florida just after my certification. This particular area was the home of the manatee, an almost extinct underwater mammal. These peaceful creatures are vegetarians, and they nurse their young.

It is not easy to actually see a manatee while diving there. I accidentally looked down under the water, while resting on the surface, and saw a large manatee cow slowly swimming, about six feet below me. I was barely able to submerge in time and dive down to touch its back just as it moved away. It was unforgettable.

As discouraged as I felt, with the boat rolling and my stomach churning, I knew that I would not give up diving, and I knew that I would get past this inconvenience with time.

My system stabilized after a few hours out of the water. We went to dinner, had a few drinks, and were exhausted, as is usually the case after two daytime dives and a night dive.

I wasn't prepared for the kind of hallucinations I would experience that night after I went to bed. Around two in the morning, I became semi-conscious. The ceiling of my room was flowing with waves just like the ocean. I was wet with cold perspiration, and the table lamp next to my bunk became the head of a white horse, it was spitting across the room making a noise like the sounds that people who chew tobacco or dip snuff make. I thought I was going insane. Although it was a difficult night, I was stabilized the next morning and dove again that day.

Like most risky activities, I had to pay a small price with physical damage and pain. But the trade off was a bargain, so I just got on with it.

After ten days under water, I had an uncontrollable urge to leave the sea and soar in the beautiful blue sky.

Part VI

UltraLight

I bought an ultralight airplane, sight unseen. It was colorfully designed like the Red Baron's World War I Bi-plane. It had black crosses on the wings, like the insignia's on the Red Baron's plane, but with bright red wings. I flew with my instructor two times before I was released to fly solo. He trained me in a dual seater with dual controls.

An ultralight airplane is little more than a hang glider with a seat and a motor. They are dangerous, but very exciting, because they fly just above the roof tops. I bought the airplane from one of my sky diving associates.

I lived in Huntsville, at the time, but I stayed in an apartment in Montgomery, because I was still in the Senate and needed to be in Montgomery much of the time.

Saturday mornings were flying mornings, if the weather was good. We would get up early, while the air was still cool, in the spring and fly out of an old cornfield in rural Montgomery County. The farmers were fascinated, and they thought we were crazy, but they enjoyed the entertainment. They would drive their pickup trucks to the edge of the cornfield to watch.

Flying an ultralight is about as close as one can get to actually free flying like a bird. The ultralight could fly from a low altitude, just above the tree tops, and up to six or seven thousand feet. I could feel and smell the air, with the wind in my face, it was exhilarating. The motor and propeller were located directly behind the pilot's seat, and the controls consisted of a stick, two foot pedals, and the accelerator. The accelerator was the handle of the control stick, much like a motorcycle accelerator in the handle bar grip. You twisted the handle in one direction to accelerate, or the other, to decelerate. It was a beautiful flying experience.

People would stand out in the fields to wave, or pull their trucks off the edge of the road to get out and watch.

Since there were no parachutes, if the engine malfunctioned, the pilot had to be prepared to land the plane as though it were a glider. There was an immediate need to spot a landing area and start the descent, because any delay could be deadly. If the plane had a structural failure, which occurred occasionally, it would instantly plunge to the ground.

I had flown two weekends in a dual ultralight, handling the controls while we were airborne, when my trainer asked me if I was ready to solo. We had just landed, and I said yes. He hopped out and said go for it.

I was excited when he told me to go for the solo. I had all the basic instructions in my head, with respect to taking off and landing, but I had never experienced the feeling alone, so I was a little apprehensive.

I turned the plane around to face the wind, took a deep breath, revved the engine all the way, and began the bumpy ride down the cornfield. As I got to the fence row, at the end of the cornfield, I pulled back on the stick and gently lifted off the ground. My heart was racing, right along with the engine. I banked to the left, and circled the field, as the farmers anxiously waited to see if I would make it.

Alone, I flew over the beautiful farm lands, the houses, and barns. I felt that sense of freedom that I had felt when my parachute opened on my first sky dive. I had overcome the fear, and I was going to survive, so I started to enjoy it.

When I came in for my first solo landing, I narrowly avoided the tops of the power lines along the road. I had pushed the stick a little too far, trying to get the nose down, and I was stunned when I realized how close the lines were to the plane and landing gear. I hardly had time to recover from the scare before the aircraft was touching the ground. My trainer ran out and yelled, "Take it up again". I wanted to get out and jump up and down and celebrate, but I followed his instructions and revved up the engine and took off again. This time I was going to get a bigger test than the power lines.

The take off was perfect, and I was beginning to get that same over-confidence that caused me to smash on the runway when I was skydiving. I tipped my wings as I soared over the curious farmers. I climbed higher and banked deeper, feeling more confident by the minute. The weather was nearly perfect on a beautiful Saturday morning.

I was actually showing off for my trainer's wife, who came out to the field every Saturday, to flirt and watch. I was smitten with her, she was pretty, slim, and sexy. There was always a hug in it for me, and she seemed more than just friendly. I sometimes had the feeling that her husband, my trainer, was aware of the attraction. All the more reason I should have been more cautious than normal. But risk was part of the adventure.

I crossed over the highway, and I could see that I was now over a small wooded area, consisting mostly of pine trees, without any clearing in sight. Suddenly, I thought I heard the engine skip, and I tensed up and listened closely. It sounded normal, but it got my attention and I immediately banked the plane and headed back toward some open terrain.

The next time the engine skipped, it shut down completely and the aircraft started to immediately lose altitude.

Again, I did exactly what I was trained NOT to do. I tried to start the engine. There was no automatic engine starter button, instead there was a rope with a wooden handle, so all I had to do was pull, in much the same fashion as starting a lawn mower. I did so, about four times as hard as I could, without success.

Now the aircraft was dropping faster, and I concentrated on my training like a laser. The rule is, that in case of engine failure, DO NOT TRY TO START THE ENGINE, but concentrate immediately on locating a land clearing and glide the plane there for a landing. Being nothing more than a glider with an engine, the plane could make a soft landing without injury, if the pilot is in control, and provided that the plane is at sufficient altitude to reach a clearing.

I spotted a clearance below where a few cows were grazing. I hoped that they would not drift into the landing area, because I had to land quickly. The silence of the ultralight without any engine noise, was really scary.

The only discernible sound was the wind cutting across the wings, and blowing in my face and ears.

Expecting to see a big crash, the farmers and everyone around the flight field, started their trucks and began driving to the cow pasture where I was headed. The dust was flying in all directions as their pickups turned on the old dirt road at the end of the cow pasture.

I narrowly missed one of the cows when I touched down. The plane bounced about three times before it came to rest. Taking a deep breath, I looked back at the engine behind my head and saw that the switch had vibrated to the "off" position. I realized that if I had known that when the engine first stopped, all I would have had to do was turn it back on and crank it up again.

I did just that, after I regained my composure. It cranked right up and I had just enough space to get airborne and fly right over the heads of all those disappointed spectators. I flew back to the landing field and over the power lines, with no trouble, and I landed about the time that they were all arriving.

I had all the excitement that I could handle on my first solo flying day. I bounded out of the plane, shouting and laughing. I jumped up and down and spun around as my friends joined me in the celebration. We passed around the bottle and hugged each other while the boom box was playing *Proud Mary.*

The instructor's wife, patting me on the shoulder, whispered in my ear that if I would meet her behind the van, she would give me a present. When the excitement settled, I eased around behind the van to meet her. She gave me an exceptional body hug and a deep kiss.

I drifted back to rejoin the crowd, realizing that once again, luck had been with me. However, I was still skeptical about how the engine switch had suddenly turned itself off.

This was yet another of the many experiences that constitute my life. Confronting fear is the fire that has always driven me.

Somewhere I read an interesting account of people who live to be in their nineties. The story was about a survey of those people, and the things that they remembered most vividly about their lives. Surprisingly it wasn't their successes or failures, but the times they took risks.

Element
8

The Last Sunday

I could see that my mother was dying. Her voice was barely more than a whisper. I could see the uncertainty and fear in her eyes.

As I held her cold, pale, hand, I could hardly believe that this was the same hand that had smashed my lips on so many occasions. Could this sweet, frightened face be the same one that glared at me in rage, and cursed me through gritted teeth when I was a child?

It was about 10 p.m. on Sunday, September 24th 1994, and the last night I would see her alive.

I had been driving from Birmingham to Huntsville every Friday, for the past two years, to visit with her in a nursing home.

I fed my mother, and read to her, throughout the weekends until late on Sunday night. I had watched her health deteriorate from week to week. These were two of the most difficult years of my life, but we became closer duing that period than we had ever been previously.

As I sat beside her hospital bed, on that last Sunday night, holding her hand, I knew that her difficult life would soon be over. She had paid dearly, having lived her entire life in a broken body. She had been born into a poor, working-class family. She was one of eight children. They lived in a small house in Paint Rock, Alabama before moving to Madison

County to get work in the cotton mills.

When she was only eighteen months old, she crawled off the back porch of their old house in Paint Rock. The house was on the edge of a small cliff, and she fell a considerable distance from the porch to the base of the cliff. The impact of the fall cut and crushed her right leg.

Her parents had little money, so they did what all poor people do when a child gets injured, they attempted to treat her at home by binding up her right leg and carrying her around until she was three years old. This home treatment allowed the torn flesh to heal, and the crushed bone to mend, but her leg was deformed, twisted, and drawn up behind her back.

Fate had dealt a normal healthy child a hard blow. At a time when most children are playfully enjoying life, she was an invalid. Her already difficult life was compounded with a crippling injury.

She walked on crutches until she was sixteen, spending most of her high school days with a leg she couldn't use.

One of the officials at her school made inquiry about medical assistance programs that could help indigent students through the County Health Department. They made arrangements for her to go to Nashville, on public assistance funds, to have her leg straightened. Ironically she was treated at the same hospital, with the same public financing program that was utilized by my father many years later. He expired there in the mid-1940s.

Somehow our intuition tells us when someone's life is over. As Kathrin had often said, people decide when they are going to die. Both my mother and I knew that this would be our last night together. I tried not to let her see my tears as I held onto her. The nurse had already told me that it was time for me to leave, but I was reluctant to go, sensing what would inevitability happen.

During my younger years, I had a rather distant association with her. I always felt that she was too busy pitying herself, because of her handicap, to have any time to care for my sister or me. I remembered that her parents treated her as an invalid, keeping her close to them as long as possible. I'm sure they suffered tremendous guilt because of her injury and their lack of funds to have her treated.

When she returned home from the Nashville Hospital, she was only sixteen, and her right leg was straight. It was about eight inches shorter than her left one, and there was no knee or joint, so the leg could not bend. She had to wear a brace, which had a shoe built on to it. The shoe was mounted on a steel seat that had four eight-inch metal extensions down to the base platform. When she walked she had to pump her entire body, swinging her right leg and brace to the front to take a step.

People, especially children, stared at her. I can still visualize her walking the two blocks from our house in the mill village to catch the bus. The kids would innocently point to her leg and call the other children's attention to it. I could see, by the pained expression on her face, the embarrassment that this handicap caused her.

As I lay there with my head resting on her bed, cherishing my last few hours with her, I felt none of the resentment that I had in the past when she constantly reminded everyone of her disadvantage. I felt nothing but love for her now, and we expressed that to each other at special times during those last two years.

The nurse touched my shoulder and brought me out of my deep thoughts, and I knew it was time to drive back to Birmingham. I gently kissed my mother on the forehead, which brought a faint smile though her eyes remained closed.

The two hour drive gave me time to recall the limited and stressful association that I, as a child, had with my mother. There were no close or loving times like the gentle affection we now shared. I did, however, remember her harsh temper and lack of patience. The only tenderness that I could recall from those childhood days came from my association with Kathrin, and occasionally from my grandmother.

As my car sped along the empty highway, I thought about my stepfather and what a dichotomy he and my father represented. My stepfather was a large, somewhat offensive, man who drank and used profanity as his preferred form of communication. In contrast, my father was a small framed man, who never indulged in liquor, nor did he use vulgar language.

The change in our home-life was a shock, and a very difficult adjustment for my sister and me. It was harder on my sister because she had no way of escape. I would simply stay away from home most of the time.

My stepfather became a much different person as he aged. In fact, instead of that loud, profane, drunk that I had known in the earlier years of their marriage, he became a helpless coward who was afraid of medical treatment, or any kind of controversy for that matter. As his health deteriorated, he progressively became more dependent upon me, not even allowing himself to be taken to the doctor unless I accompanied him. I felt nothing but pity as I looked into those frightened, and somewhat pleading eyes, when we would prepare for the short trip to his doctor. It was a drastic change from those earlier days when he boasted about all of his conquests.

Louis made his living as a projectionist, working at movie theaters in a little room above the balcony called "the booth", where the projectors were located. He kept the machines running without interruption, including previews and cartoons.

Brief through it was, I enjoyed that part of my life,   when I lived with my mother and stepfather. My mother would take my sister and me to the theater, almost daily, during those few months when we lived in Mobile, Alabama. We would catch the bus around seven in the evening and go to the movie. We didn't have to pay for the tickets to get in, and we would sit in the balcony.

I watched all of those movies of the forties. Even now, while watching them on the classic movie channels on television, it always transports me back to that time in the balcony.

I must have seen all of the movies of that era, and I knew the names of all of the actors. My stepfather knew the names of all the supporting movie stars, and he was a reservoir of information when it came to the actors' private lives. He had a remarkable knowledge of movie memorabilia.

I recalled that most of the time, when we watched the movies in the balcony, I couldn't stay awake till closing. I would inevitably succumb to the hypnotic projector light and sounds blending with the delicious smell of buttery popcorn. It was irresistible, so I would wrap my body around the arms of the theater seats and go to sleep only to wake up as the house lights came on. I would then stumble to my stepfather's car to go home.

While submerged in my deep reminiscing, I was unaware that I had already driven half the distance back to Birmingham. As I passed through Cullman, Alabama, I remembered traveling this same route by bus just a few months after my mother's marriage to Louis.

At that time, bus travel was the main source of transportation between cities. The bus driver was like a ship captain, completely in charge of the bus and passengers. The bus stopped in practically every little town from north to south Alabama. He would shout, "Araaaab (Arab), "Oneeeeeeontaaa (Oneonta)" when the bus stopped in Arab and Oneonta, Alabama. Sometimes he would stop the bus to allow passengers to use the restroom, or just open the bus door to pick up someone, depending upon whether the bus was on schedule.

I witnessed my first exciting sexual encounter that night on the long bus trip.

I was sitting in the aisle seat with my sister, who was by the window sleeping, my mother and stepfather sat back a few rows behind me. Across the aisle from me sat a man and a woman, not traveling together, but sitting beside each other. He had a half-pint of whiskey in his coat and they were sharing it and touching heavily. I pretended to be asleep so that they would not detect my watching them. He ran his hand inside her dress and fondled her breasts. Then he slid his hand up her dress, causing her dress to rise halfway up her thighs. I experienced my first sexual arousal watching them.

The bus stopped on the highway to pick up a passenger and the lights came on, allowing me a much better view. Lipstick was smeared all over both their faces and she attempted to pull her skirt down.

I learned, from overhearing their conversation earlier, that she was a schoolteacher. I had also noticed that some teenage girls who got off the bus earlier had called her by name, I assumed they knew her from class. When the driver closed the bus doors and began the trip again, he left the lights on for an unusually long time. The man who had been fondling the woman began saying "Lights out driver". He must have said it four or five times before the driver finally turned off the lights. When the lights went off the couple resumed their sexual exploration. The woman now sounded drunk, she was getting a little loud and slurring her words.

As my mind exploded from my imagination, he slid his hand around the back of her head and pulled her face down into his lap. She immediately resisted and tried to sit up, but he was determined and attempted to force her down again. This time she said, loud enough for the driver of the bus to hear, "It stinks down there". The driver then turned the lights on and kept them on until the teacher staggered down the bus aisle and got off at her stop a short time later.

I didn't realize it at the time, but that was just the beginning of new experiences for me. I would later be exposed to things that I had never even thought about. In fact, I reached my first sexual climax just a few months following the bus ride. It happened, of all places, in a tree!

A new friend, who lived in the same public housing project that I did, was with me. We lived a few blocks from Vigor School. There was a trail behind the school that led to the housing project. The trail was in a wooded area with large trees lining the pathway.

Walking along the pathway from school, my friend and I decided to climb into a big Oak tree to watch and listen to girls, who often walked home through the wooded area.

My friend had a severe urge to urinate while we were in the tree. Since we were completely concealed in the thick leaves and branches, he did it while standing on a tree limb.

A small group of girls was approaching the tree as the urine rained down through the leaves. The sound of the girls voices stopped abruptly as they peered up into the tree, trying to locate the source of the water that was now splattering on the ground several feet away from where they were standing.

I think the girls caught a glimpse of my friend through the thick leaves, because they began to giggle and laugh when they realized what was happening. The sound of their voices and laughter floated up through the thick foliage like butterflies, drifting and dancing on the soft summer breeze.

It excited and aroused me further, as I continued to listen to the sound of their voices, my groin began to ache. I felt as though I would explode. The more they giggled, the tighter I gripped myself. Suddenly, I experienced waves of pulsing, throbbing, pleasure engulfing me. It was a sexual release that I had never felt before. I almost fell out of the tree.

It was my very first climax; I referred to as a "feel good", because I didn't know what a climax was at the time.

Slowly coming back to the present, I felt as though the bus trip had happened in another lifetime. Even that short time in Mobile seemed like a dream.

I wondered what Alabama Village looked like now. It was a public housing project near Prichard, Alabama, and my home through that summer and into the fall.

My home life in Mobile was miserable, except for the movies, because I couldn't adjust to my stepfather's lifestyle and his ever-present profanity. But I enjoyed being with my friends that lived in the housing project. We stayed outside from dawn till dusk, so that I didn't have to be around my stepfather. He usually went to work about three in the afternoon and worked until the theater closed, which was around eleven.

The city lights of Birmingham brought me back to the present, it was almost midnight. Exhausted, I couldn't shake the feeling that I had seen my mother alive for the last time. I put some soft music on, and had two glasses of sherry, finally drifting off to sleep, only to be jolted awake by the phone ringing at four in the morning. The call was to tell me that my mother was gone. I asked if she had experienced any pain, and the nurse said, "No, I don't think she even opened her eyes again after you left, she looked peaceful."

I sat on my balcony, overlooking the city until daybreak, reminiscing about my life with her, before and after my stepfather. I remembered how much she liked Mobile, but how awkward she seemed when my stepfather would use profanity around my sister and me. How difficult it must have been, I thought, being handicapped physically, and having the responsibility for two children while living with such a man. I remembered how I used to plot my escape. I intended to find my way back to Kathrin's place, but before I could initiate my plan, we had to leave Mobile.

We moved, just ahead of the bill collectors, into a boarding house in East Gadsden. We lived in rooms upstairs over a chicken processing plant. Aside from the stench of chickens, it reminded me of my Grandmother's boarding house. These boarders were not mill workers, they were all employees of Revis Chicken Plant that was located downstairs.

A man named Revis owned the building, boarding house, and chicken plant. His wife cooked all the meals, as did my grandmother, and we again ate at a big table with the boarders sitting around.

The upstairs had a living room area for everyone who lived there. The hallway ran the length of the building, and it had rooms on both sides. The bathroom, at the end of the hall, was for everyone, except the Revis' family, who had their own facility. Mr. Revis allowed my mother and my sister to use their bathroom. My sister and I slept in one room that had two half beds, and my mother and stepfather slept in the adjoining room. It was especially hard for my mother to climb the steps, in the old boarding house, with her right leg that couldn't bend.

Those close quarters were stressful, especially when my stepfather got drunk, loud, and abusive, which he did almost every payday.

As I stood on my deck in the early morning, I gazed at the silhouette of Sloss Furnace, and thought of my first job in Gadsden at the age of ten. I could almost smell the chicken guts again. It was an unforgettable stench that lingered in my nostrils, even after my shift.

I recalled the day I asked Mr. Revis if I could work for him, and he said he would give me a try. He paid me ten cents an hour, and I stood on a Coca-Cola case and worked on the processing line.

Living in a commercial area, rather than residential area, eliminated the possibility of having other children my age around for companionship, so my friends became the men who worked in the processing plant. I hung around with them as much as I could.

I worked almost every position on the processing line. The most difficult one required me to disembowel the dead chicken. The first day, I worked that position, I had to be excused five times to go to the toilet to vomit. Soon there was nothing left to throw-up, but I was determined to get past it, hoping the other guys didn't notice. They did though because they would ask me if I was all right. I always responded that I was fine. After all, I had my first job, and I was determined to keep it.

One of my favorite co-workers in the plant was named Howard. He did everything, including slitting the chickens' throats, and driving the delivery truck.

After the chickens were dressed, they were delivered to the local restaurants, grocery stores, etc. Sometimes I would go along with him to deliver chickens. I welcomed this, because I could get out of the stinking plant and breathe again. Another reason was that I also enjoyed hearing Howard's stories about his life and experiences, which included everything from his times in jail to his vast sexual escapades. Much of it, I'm sure, was fabricated, but I liked it anyway. We worked in the plant everyday from seven in the morning until seven in the evening, with the exception of Saturdays when we got off at noon.

Saturday afternoon was a big deal, because we had money from our paychecks. I felt as much an adult as the men I worked with, nevertheless, we would separate on Saturday, because I was too young to go with them to the beer joints. How ironic I would think, in just a few short months I would be back at Kathrin's where bootleg moonshine was served while I watched.

The siren of an ambulance in the early morning mist brought me back to the present.

I looked out across the skyline as dawn was beginning to break, and I could see the Jefferson-Hillman Hospital, where my sister was taken to have electrical shock treatments administered. I wondered if the drastic change in her life, after my mother married Louis, was the reason. She was about thirteen at the time, and I suspected that she was sexually abused.

She always looked relieved after the electrical shock treatments. She seemed at peace when she left the Hospital for the two-hour drive back to Huntsville. She was asleep in the back of the car within fifteen minutes, and usually slept for most of the next three days.

I wondered if my mother had any idea, or if she chose not to see anything. I saw Louis fondle my sister once, when we lived in the boarding house in Gadsden, while my mother was in the room. He kissed my sister, and touched her breasts. My mother acted as though she didn't see. My sister was repulsed and pushed him away.

I wasn't around to witness anymore episodes of molestation,

197

because I left them to live with Kathrin.

The sadness of my mother's death came back to me, and I wondered how my sister would take the news. I had to call her that morning because I didn't think she would have known; the hospital was directed to notify me first. I knew that she was especially close to our mother, because she had always lived near her. She was still very fragile, having never adjusted to the change in her early life at home.

I dreaded to make the calls, and I wanted to wait until I was sure everyone was up before disturbing their night. As I had expected, my sister lost control and it was all I could do to reason with her. She was still very fragile, both physically and emotionally.

Even though she made my life miserable when we were younger, I still felt much compassion for her. Those few years difference in our ages seemed to fuel her wanting to take her anger and resentment out on me. I didn't realize, at the time, that she had such intense dislike for males.

She hammered me with negative remarks. She seemed to think that we were all disgusting pigs. It hurt my feelings too think that she felt that way about me. Her actions, in my early formative years, had a major impact on my self-esteem, making me very shy and reserved around girls. I carried the emotional wounds, inflicted by her hate and disgust for men, throughout most of my adolescent years.

The funeral was sad and simple. I was relieved that my mother had finally shed her handicapped body.

Within an eighteen-month period I had lost both Kathrin and my mother, and I wondered when the pain would ease.

During that time, I had spent most of my weekends with my biological mother, so I decided to share a weekend with both of them.

I felt that I had neglected Kathrin, and it was troubling my spirit. It had been over six months since I had visited her.

In anticipation of my trip to Huntsville, I had a birthday present for Kathrin, it was a red sweater, and a birthday card. I was also going to get her roses. She loved the color red.

I called to let her know when I would be arriving. Kathrin's sister answered the phone and told me that she had passed away two weeks earlier. She said that Kathrin didn't want anyone to call me, because she knew that I was occupied with my mother. I was shattered. I didn't even know that she was sick.

That weekend was the most painful that I had ever experienced, even more painful than when I returned from France. I didn't go to Huntsville, in fact, I didn't go anywhere. I stayed home and sank into a deep depression, playing Robert Johnson and Jimmy Reed music, and grieving.

Mother and Kathrin, the first and the last, it seemed that destiny had spared Kathrin from a long illness, which in turn spared me from the lingering torture of watching them both die.

While that time allowed me to mend a battered relationship with my biological mother, and heal some emotional wounds, it caused me to lose Kathrin without having those last special days with her.

I'm still, just getting on with it.

Summary

Some seemingly insignificant incidents in my life turned out to be major life experiences. For instance, a simple five-minute reprimand from my father about a derogatory reference, with respect to an African American man adjusted both my attitude and sensitivity towards the differences in human beings from that day forward. It was an adjustment that allowed an open and ultimately very close relationship with an African American woman. This synchronism makes me wonder about so many other aspects of my life.

* I wonder if I would have met Kathrin if my future stepfather hadn't decided on that particular Saturday that he wanted a shot of moonshine.

* I wonder if I would have had an open and accepting soul for Kathrin if my father hadn't adjusted my essence when he heard my use of the term "Nigra" when referring to an African American hobo on that particular Sunday afternoon.

* I wonder if I would have ever lived in Europe and fell in love with a French girl if I hadn't been selected on that unusual day in April for an interview with the Student Exchange Panel.

* I wonder if I would have gone to college if I hadn't been approaching an intersection that night in Nashville at the instant a pickup truck ran a stop sign, colliding with my car and ending a lost year with Ruby.

*   I wonder if I would have ran for public office if my resentment for the "establishment" hadn't been compounded on that day in downtown Huntsville, when I was kicked out of the YMCA as a "Lint Head".

*   I wonder if I would have been George Wallace's adversary if he hadn't humiliated me during that first meeting in the presence of my colleagues.

*   I wonder if I would have become an entrepreneur and developer if I hadn't become disillusioned with politics.

*   I wonder if I would have ever confronted my fears if I hadn't needed the edge.

*   I wonder if I would have ever needed the edge if I hadn't have experienced life at Kathrin's and in the mill village.

*   I wonder if I would have survived a major business development failure if I hadn't been indoctrinated with Kathrin's philosophy that "You can't lose when you start with nothin."

*   I wonder if I would have been so fearless if I hadn't been molded by Kathrin's wisdom.

*   I wonder if my stepfather would have ever been involved in my life if my father hadn't have been playing softball on that Wednesday night when his kidney was injured, resulting in his death.

*   I wonder if I would have been here if one of the five hundred million sperms released by my father into my mother's womb that special night in January hadn't successfully penetrated and fertilized a single egg.

*   I wonder if we, as humans, know that we start on this planet beating a five hundred million to one odd. I wonder if we realize that the day we took our first breath, we had already beaten more odds than all the lotteries in the world combined. I wonder what my next life will be like . . .